*To my early mentors, who touched my heart and mind:*
*Zora and John Selby, Krishnamurti, Humphrey Osmond,*
*Chuck Kelley, Osho, and Alan Watts*

# EXPAND
# THIS
# MOMENT

## ALSO BY JOHN SELBY

*Quiet Your Mind*
*Tapping the Source*
*Seven Masters, One Path*
*Executive Genius*
*Listening with Empathy*
*Let Love Find You*
*Kundalini Awakening*
*Take Charge of Your Mind*
*Secrets of a Good Night's Sleep*
*Jesus for the Rest of Us*
*Conscious Healing*
*The Conscious Capitalist*
*Belly Talk*
*Finding Each Other*
*Power Point*
*Meditation*
*Fathers*
*Solitude*
*The Mahee Vision* (novel)
*Shooting Angels* (novel)
*10% Max* (novel)

# EXPAND
# THIS
# MOMENT

focused meditations
to quiet your mind,
brighten your mood
& set yourself free

# JOHN SELBY
with Birgitta Steiner

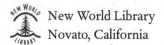

New World Library
Novato, California

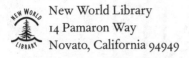

New World Library
14 Pamaron Way
Novato, California 94949

Text design and typography by Tona Pearce Myers

Library of Congress Cataloging-in-Publication Data
Selby, John, date.
 Expand this moment : focused meditations to quiet your mind, brighten your mood & set yourself free / John Selby with Birgitta Steiner.
    p.   cm.
ISBN 978-1-57731-970-2 (pbk. : alk. paper)
1. Meditation. I. Steiner, Birgitta. II. Title.
BL627.S456 2011
204'.35—dc22                                    2011000449

First printing, April 2011
ISBN 978-1-57731-970-2
Printed in Canada on 100% postconsumer-waste recycled paper

New World Library is a proud member of the Green Press Initiative.

10  9  8  7  6  5  4  3  2  1

*Empty your mind of all thoughts.*
*Let your heart be at peace.*
*Each separate being in the universe*
*returns to the common source.*
*Returning to the source is serenity.*
*Then you can deal with whatever life brings you.*

—— LAO-TZU

# CONTENTS

# WHY EXPAND THIS MOMENT?

*When you become content with what you have*
*and rejoice in the way things are,*
*when you realize that there is nothing lacking,*
*then the whole world belongs to you.*

— LAO-TZU

It's hard to believe that I've turned sixty-four and am only just now fulfilling a challenge given to me way back when I was twenty-four. The challenge — from the philosopher and meditation expert Alan Watts — was to study the world's meditation traditions as a psychologist from the inside out; identify the underlying psychological process common to all those traditions; and then go out and teach this process to any who might want to learn it.

I was in grad school at Berkeley in the early 1970s when I received this challenge. I assumed I could fulfill the research project as part of my doctoral thesis, never suspecting that my life would get caught up for decades in what proved to be a seemingly endless quest. Throughout the rest of the seventies, then the eighties, and into the nineties, the search continued to unfold like a psychological and spiritual detective plot, loaded with half-hidden clues and convoluted insights, many dead-end detours, and dozens of invaluable encounters with remarkable men and women.

At first I thought the challenge would be an intellectual academic adventure. But I discovered step-by-step that I was looking for meaningful answers in all the wrong places. In fact my eventual discovery of the twelve Focus Phrases that make up the heart of what I'm going to teach you in this book did not come to me through scientific research and logical deduction. Instead the breakthrough came as an unexpected realization that aimed my focus beyond my personal ego and academic perspectives toward a much broader, more universal understanding.

To be honest, that realization emerged only when I finally broke down altogether on all fronts, hit bottom emotionally and intellectually, and surrendered. The words of the spiritual teacher Krishnamurti, whom I knew from my very early years, state lucidly how my insights came: "The mind must be empty, in order to see clearly."

## INFLOW OF INSIGHT

My breakdown happened one night without warning, as I returned home from an unsuccessful trip to raise money to keep a floundering online therapy project afloat. Reaching my quiet country home in Kauai, Hawaii, I simply fell apart emotionally and mentally, overwhelmed with a sense of total confusion and despair. I went physically limp and almost blind as my inner consciousness dimmed and then went out altogether.

A visiting friend with medical knowledge was afraid I'd suffered a stroke or had a brain tumor. But as I dropped down into blackness, my wife luckily didn't freak out and throw me in the hospital. Somehow we both knew that something deeper was happening, a weird new flow that must be surrendered to.

For hours I experienced mostly blackness, no sensation, no thoughts, nothing. I was simply there, on my back in bed, knocked flat. Then, in the midst of that nothingness, I suddenly started to experience my own spark of consciousness naturally reemerging, expanding all on its own without my ego in any way instigating or directing the expansion. Without "me" doing anything at all, I began to passively experience a point of awareness inside my nose, and then a sudden sensation of air rushing through my nostrils.

Ah...life!

And then — blankness again.

During the next hour or two I went through this core process several times, suddenly rising up into the experience of the air flowing in and out of my nose, then dropping into blackness again. At some point I found my awareness maintaining itself rather than dropping away. Then, in a second expansion, my bubble of awareness grew to include both the sensation of breath in my nose, and the sensations generated by the muscular contractions and expansions of breathing in my chest and my belly.

For a while, my awareness collapsed into nothingness again...and then effortlessly began to move through the same progression of expansion. This perceptual ebb and flow continued in the same basic progression until, at some point, an even more remarkable inner experience came to me. I became suddenly aware of my whole physical body all at once, here in the eternal now.

These intense perceptual and emotional experiences marked the organic origins of the first part of the meditation process I'm going to teach you. Of course, being aware of one's breathing is certainly not a new meditation discovery. Breath awareness has been, from the beginning, the foundation of most meditation methods throughout the world. What was unique for me was the direct inner experience showing me exactly how consciousness naturally expands.

The experience was so strong that I knew that this three-step perceptual expansion (feeling the air flowing through my nose, feeling the movements in my chest and belly with each breath, and feeling my awareness expand to include my whole body at once in the present moment) was a root psychological-meditative process.

## INNER VOICE

People often report the emergence, during meditation, of an inner voice that one way or another communicates deep insights to them that become part of their everyday awareness. When I was very young I would occasionally hear a loving interior voice. This inner voice went away when I was eight years old, and returned only occasionally during deep meditation or moments of extreme emotion. This same voice returned to me anew during my breakdown. During the next few days, as I experienced again and again the expansion of my awareness and its collapse, my inner voice would quietly and succinctly describe what was happening to me.

I heard the voice say, "I feel the air flowing in and out of my nose."

Then with the second expansion, the voice said, "I also feel the movements in my chest and belly as I breathe."

Then came the words "I'm aware of my whole body at once, here in this present moment."

At first these core statements might seem obvious and even simplistic — they're just sentences describing what I was experiencing. But I soon realized that these words were extremely powerful elicitor phrases: whenever I wanted to move through the same expansion process and wake up to the present moment as I did that day, all I had to do was remember to say these Focus Phrases to myself in the proper order. Almost instantly my whole being would respond as I guided myself through the expansion process.

## FOCUS PHRASES

During the week of my breakdown and awakening, nine more Focus Phrases rose spontaneously into my mind. Each of these proved to concisely evoke a vital psychological process. The twelve Focus Phrases are divided into three phases, as follows:

### PHASE I. ZEN AWAKENING

1. I choose to enjoy this moment.

2. I feel the air flowing in and out of my nose.

3. I also feel the movements in my chest and belly as I breathe.

4. I'm aware of my whole body at once,
here in this present moment.

These first four Focus Phrases shift your attention from thoughts about the past and future to a clear present-moment perceptual experience, naturally quieting your mind and inducing a heightened state of peace, pleasure, and compassion.

## PHASE 2. EMOTIONAL HEALING

5. I am ready to experience the feelings in my heart.

6. I let go of all my stress and worries, and feel peaceful inside.

7. I accept everyone I know, just as they are.

8. I honor and love myself just as I am.

Almost everybody brings both a busy mind and a bunch of emotions into a meditation experience. This second group of four Focus Phrases helps you transcend the primary emotional blocks to deep meditative awakening and insight.

## PHASE 3. INSIGHT MODE

9. I am open to receive.

10. I feel connected with my Source.

11. I'm here to serve, to love, to prosper, and to enjoy myself.

12. I am ready to act with courage and integrity.

The first eight Focus Phrases (which you can move through in just a couple of minutes once you become familiar with the process) fully prepare you for deep meditation. The next two Focus Phrases, numbers 9 and 10, aim your attention directly toward your inner core of being, and help you open yourself to receive whatever meditative experience might occur at that moment. You can then move on to the final two Focus Phrases, which bring you out of meditation. You can remain in deep meditation for as long as you like.

Each time you pause and move through this process, you'll find that the experience is new. You're opening your heart and soul to receive spiritual flow from the infinite Source — and no one can possibly predict what will come to you.

One thing you can predict about a meditative experience is this: as you quiet your mind and tune in to your spiritual presence, you will feel less anxiety and stress, and more peace and joy. Meditation is a conscious switch from thoughts that generate negative emotions and tensions in the body toward acceptance, insight, and freedom.

Krishnamurti spoke of the uniqueness of the experience:

> *To begin to meditate*
> *you must take a plunge into the water*
> *not knowing how to swim.*
> *The beauty of meditation is that*
> *you never know where you are,*
> *where you are going,*
> *what the end is.*
>
> *Meditation is freedom from thought —*
> *meditation is an explosion of intelligence.*

## LEADING A HORSE TO WATER

Being a pragmatic psychologist as well as an inquisitive person, I naturally had to ask myself: where exactly had these Focus Phrases come from? Did I access them by somehow temporarily becoming a human channel for the spiritual presence we usually call God? Or did my intuitive-integrative brain, after so much research and reflection, finally cough up the compressed logical resolution to my lifelong query? Or was there perhaps a more obscure, esoteric source that I'd tapped into?

Well, perhaps all of the above. Whatever the source, what I do know is that, since these twelve Focus Phrases came to me a decade ago, they've been my daily meditation and the primary psychological tool I teach to my students and employ with my therapy clients. After so many years of searching, I became a finder. It was a relief. Here's how I summarize the hopeful, deeper intent of the Focus Phrases: like a unifying scientific formula that's both short and potent, this collection of phrases is a complete process to help you regularly reawaken present-moment awareness, heal emotional aches and pains, encourage meditative surrender, and stimulate intuitive insight.

So yes, I'm a fan; but please — don't take my word for any of this. My intent isn't to use words to convince you of the power and beauty of these twelve elicitor statements, and certainly not to program your imagination with lofty visions of spiritual experiences that the Focus Phrases might induce. My intent in offering this book is simply to help you aim your attention more successfully toward whatever unique experiences these Focus Phrases stimulate in your own inner universe.

My role in this is that of teacher, not self-proclaimed enlightened guru. I grew up on a cattle ranch where everybody was equal — and I seem to still live in that world a great deal, despite having gone off to the Ivy League and hopped through a lot of academic hoops. The only difference between you and me regarding meditation is that I've been paid for thirty years to focus my attention on the phenomenon of meditation, and naturally I've got a bit to say about what I've found. Beyond that — equal beings, you and me. That's how we stay free.

In his work training animals, my granddad used the old adage "You can lead a horse to water but you can't make it drink."

This metaphor also makes sense spiritually — a teacher can point your attention in directions that have proven powerful. But each student must choose to aim his or her attention in those directions, to discover their unique experiential truth.

Like me, my clients and students have found that each time you say one of the twelve Focus Phrases, you move through that Focus Phrase's particular psychological and spiritual portal. And each new time you say the Focus Phrase and move through that portal, your focused attention, current desires and needs, and other present-moment factors will stimulate a new experience of who knows what — healing, love, power, discovery, or maybe pure fun and joy. Remember, you can do this meditation equally well at a party and in a Tibetan cave — and that's great freedom!

My understanding is that focused consciousness, when aided by psychologically astute elicitor statements, helps move you into whatever deep, rich, significant, and important awakening — an *Aha!* or *Oh yeah!* or *Ah so!* inner experience — comes to you, as your individual mind plugs into the Universal Mind. As one of my Hawaiian teachers used to remind us over and over again: "Energy flows where attention goes. You get what you ask for. So aim your attention carefully, with clear intent."

## SHORT-FORM MEDITATION

Traditional meditation requires that you discipline yourself to sit quietly for at least half an hour each day, preferably in the same place, so that you can move deeply into a quiet, calm, insightful experience on a regular basis. Traditional meditation evolved out of a reclusive monastic lifestyle in which people gave up secular life and retreated into a routine that gave them loads of time free to sit and meditate. This tradition continues, and I highly value its ongoing presence in the world. I spent a number of years in ashrams and meditative communities and learned a great deal in the process.

However, I prefer being more in the buzz — I love a busy life filled with creative work, interpersonal involvement, time with my family, and time outdoors. At the same time, I do need deep inner peace, emotional well-being, energetic balance, creative power, and spiritual guidance and nurturing. And I don't want them for just half an hour a day — I want and need them all the time.

My solution to this universal dilemma is what I call short-form meditation. I know full well that there are particular spiritual qualities of consciousness that come to me only when I sit for half an hour in deep meditation. Sometimes I love taking time to do just that. The daily practice I describe here allows for wonderful extended meditation, but it is also equally well suited for short dips into deep meditation. After a few weeks of practice, you'll be able to move through the twelve Focus Phrases of the practice in just three minutes — and benefit remarkably from that short but potent experience.

One of the spiritual teachers I learned a great deal from was an Indian fellow named Bhagwan Rajneesh, who later changed his name to Osho. He described meditation with broad strokes:

*Meditation is aware consciousness.*
*It is an opening, where everything becomes sacred —*
*just taking a bath, making love,*
*eating food, going to sleep. . . .*
*In meditation wherever you look is God*
*and whatever you do, you do with God.*

In this spirit, let's do what we can to bring meditation into every nook and cranny of our lives. For instance, how can we infuse a meditative perspective into the middle of a busy workday? In *Executive Genius* and *Take Charge of Your Mind*, I outlined how an entire corporation can insert three-minute meditative breaks into each hour for each employee and, in so doing, boost all levels of performance, creativity, empathy, and safety. In the last chapter of this book, I've outlined that same process for you to apply at work.

We can also infuse a meditative perspective into family and intimate relations. Too often we get caught up in negative emotions and reactions that damage our friendships and family bonds. We'll explore how you can insert just one key Focus Phrase into a situation, and generate healing and communication.

In any situation, just by holding, for instance, the first Focus Phrase, "I choose to enjoy this moment," in your mind as you go about your day, you can actively transform your life experience for the better. Try it right now: "I choose to enjoy this moment."

## REMEMBER TO REMEMBER

Almost all people want to move their lives more fully in the twelve directions that the Focus Phrases highlight, but most of the time we "forget to remember" to focus our attention on these positive directions. What to do?

Luckily we live during a high-tech period when we can readily turn computer circuits into spiritual aids. I long considered computer technology a diversion and even a negative influence on spiritual awareness. Only in the past five years or so have my eyes been opened, and my heart as well, to the amazing potential of the Internet to help us remember to regularly enter meditation mode for whatever time we have at a given moment.

My wife, Birgitta, and I have recently developed several multifaceted online systems that you can access for free to help you remember to remember, and to guide you effortlessly through this practice until it becomes second nature. On your computer or cell phone, the Internet can offer a lifeline, delivering exactly the reinforcement you will need in order to master the Focus Phrases step-by-step and continue to employ them, regardless of where you are or what you're doing.

Feel free anytime to visit www.johnselby.com or www.tap pingdaily.org, where you can access video experiences and online classes to learn the daily practice in an enjoyable format. We're also developing applications and computer reinforcement programs that will remind you periodically to pause for a quick meditative uplift. And we'll be launching an online community where you can share your experiences and meet other people exploring the daily practice. I welcome you to this new approach to becoming master of your own mind and focusing your power of attention regularly in ways that help you fulfill your deeper aspirations.

*Meditation is the inner process*
*of quietly shifting your perspective*
*so that you witness what is real*
*and thus nurture your soul.*

By the way, this is the first book I've written using voice-recognition software. Rather than pounding away at the keyboard, I'm sitting here in my easy chair quietly talking to you as we engage in reflecting on deep themes and meditative tools that you'll want to take time to fully master. At the end of each chapter, and at the end of a unit in a chapter, make sure to give yourself breathing space. Look up, pause from reading for a minute (or a day, or longer), and see what's going on inside yourself as a result of what you've just read.

In this spirit, you might want to shift in to experiential mode now. I've mentioned the power of tuning into the experience of your breathing — see what happens in the next moments when you pause after reading this paragraph and say to yourself:

*I feel the air flowing in and out of my nose.*

Allow these elicitor words to direct your attention to the air flowing in and the air flowing out. You are right here right now, alert and alive... tuning in to your own presence in the eternal present and becoming open to a new experience.

CHAPTER ONE

# ENJOY THIS MOMENT

*When you are walking or bathing,*
*eating or doing whatever*
*be aware of your breath —*
*that is meditation.*

*Be aware of the ingoing*
*and the outgoing of the breath,*
*the rhythm and the process.*
*Your mind will become silent*
*because your total mind is engaged*
*in witnessing the breathing.*

— OSHO

I drove into town this morning to see the skin doctor about a curious little growth on my scalp. Here in Hawaii we're alert to skin cancer because of all the sunlight we indulge in year-round. An acquaintance died a while back because he ignored a skin condition that was indeed melanoma, and so it was natural that I found myself sitting tensely while awaiting the doctor's verdict. Moreover, my brother went to the doctor six months ago complaining of a headache that wouldn't go away, and he was diagnosed with terminal brain cancer — so of course my mind was caught up in worst-scenario anxieties about the new lump on my head.

I'm sure you know this basic life situation, where your future is uncertain and you fixate on your fear-based apprehensions. All sense of joy in the present moment seems to collapse when anxious forebodings dominate the mind, messing with your emotions, constricting your breathing, and fogging your thoughts.

In one way, I'm lucky when it comes to breaking free from such worrying. After all, I get paid to focus day in and day out on discovering and testing new methods for shifting from feeling bad to feeling good. My life study has been meditation, which is in essence a cognitive process for letting go of fear-based emotional contractions and entering a more fulfilling, compassionate, creative, and harmonious state of mind.

So, when I realized I was making myself suffer while awaiting the doctor, I remembered to practice what I preach. I did what I hope you'll start doing — I brought to mind the first of the twelve Focus Phrases I'm going to teach you, and said silently to myself on my next exhale:

*I choose to enjoy this moment.*

First I said to myself, "I choose...," which enabled me to assume control of my own mind.

Then I said "to enjoy...," which specified where I chose to aim my attention — at enjoyment.

Then came the object of my focus, "this moment...," which aimed my attention at the immediate sensory events happening inside and around me right then.

The result was that my awareness instantly popped away from fearful imaginations about the future, toward whatever enjoyable sensations were present at the moment. By filling my mind with words of positive intent, I was able to turn away from the fearful chatter running in the back of my mind, and reconnect with ongoing sensory events happening right then inside my body.

You'll soon discover that, as I described in the introduction, whenever you shift your attention back to what's happening in the present moment, you naturally tune in first to your own breath. This shift is ideal because, as other researchers and I confirmed in perceptual studies we did some years ago at the National Institutes of Health, as soon as you focus on the sensation of air flowing in and out of your nose, all thoughts tend to simply fade away and stop. This instant quieting of the mind in turn generates relief from anxious imaginations and emotions.

*Regain your vital presence*
*as a participant in the here and now.*
*This is where all sensation and enjoyment*
*actually take place.*

And indeed, as I sat there in the doctor's cubicle, my sensory attention woke up when I said to myself, "I choose to enjoy this moment," tuned in to my breathing, and let go of upsetting memories and forebodings that'd been grabbing at me. As I took a good breath of air, I spontaneously stretched a little and woke up good feelings in my body. Just then, the doctor came in, took a look at my lump, and told me that the growth was totally benign. There was in reality nothing to worry about.

## NO MORE TORTURE CHAMBERS

If we're honest with ourselves, most of us will admit we tend to run torture chambers inside our own minds. We spend part of our lives tormenting ourselves with worries about the future — fearful imaginings and forebodings that almost never become reality. Think back over your life and consider the vast

number of times you've worried yourself sick about some potentially negative financial, health, or relationship situation that
never came to pass — or if it did, it generated much less emotional suffering than all your worrying did.

Several of the Focus Phrases you'll be learning are aimed
specifically at giving you the power to regularly short-circuit
your habitual anxiety habits. The first Focus Phrase by itself
can often do the job, once you practice a bit, by helping you
temporarily refocus your attention away from thoughts about
the past and future. By returning your attention to the experiential present moment, you will be able to relax, tune in to your
sensory presence, and more times than not, thoroughly enjoy
your here-and-now experience.

Most of your waking moments take place in safe and enjoyable situations. Maybe now and then you are forced to deal with
real danger and physical suffering, but you'll find that usually,
when you refocus on your present-moment experience, you are
indeed free to enjoy the moment rather than suffer.

*It's the culturally ingrained habit*
*of fearfully imagining negative future possibilities*
*that generates most of our suffering.*

And you do have a clear choice each new moment: You can
focus on negative anxious thoughts, uncomfortable or painful sensations, depressing guilt-ridden memories, or anxiety-
provoking future imaginations. Or you can focus on any of
the vast assortment of positive sensations, creative flashes, em-
pathetic emotions, and uplifting thoughts that make you feel
good, confident, open, bright, and yes, happy.

When you choose between anxiety and enjoyment, there's
really no reason to choose anxiety. In fact, when you see clearly

that you have the choice, there's hardly any choice to be made. The same basic logic applies to all other negative mental habits, such as heaping guilt and blame on your head, judging others overmuch, thinking thoughts that make you feel depressed or angry or wronged, and so on. You do have the power to choose to quiet such thoughts and shift your attention to the pleasure of the present moment.

## BREATH-ASSISTED EMOTIONAL RECOVERY

Once you get good at this process, 80 to 90 percent of the time you'll probably find that you can say "I choose to enjoy this moment..." and immediately feel a positive response in the direction of letting go of emotional constrictions inside you. However, maybe 10 to 20 percent of the time you might find yourself seriously caught up in bad feelings that simply won't go away. What to do?

When this happens, you'll want to shift to an alternate meditation in which you simply sit quietly and focus on your breathing experience, and at the same time focus wherever in your body you feel emotional or physical discomfort. For five to ten minutes, do nothing else — just open up and experience what happens.

Psychologically, and spiritually as well, there does seem to exist a natural emotional-healing mechanism within you that knows the wisdom of aiming healing attention, acceptance, and love toward an old emotional wound. Your challenge is to hold your attention on your breathing and on your inner pain, at the same time, for however long needed. Step by step you will "breathe away" the cause of any discomfort that stands between you and feeling good.

Perhaps at some point you'll have a flash of memory from early childhood that touches the source of your recurring emotional pain. Perhaps you'll suddenly cry a bit, or even laugh spontaneously, and release your pain. If you use this method devotedly, you'll learn to heal chronic emotional hurt and contraction.

Sometimes after such a healing session, you'll go on about your day; to the extent that you remain aware of your breathing, the healing process will continue apace. At other times, after pausing to focus on breath-assisted emotional recovery, you'll want to continue with the rest of the Focus Phrases, several of which directly augment the emotional healing and recovery process. If you want more specific guidance and insight into this particular process for core emotional healing, please visit TappingDaily.org.

## MY FIRST TEACHER

I often talk about my grandfather as my first spiritual teacher, and about the Indian master Krishnamurti, who lived half-time in my hometown and was a voice in my ear from early childhood on. But probably the deepest influence on my life was my grandmother Zora Percy Selby, known to me and all twenty-seven of my cousins as Granny. This quiet woman touched my heart very early at levels much deeper than words can communicate.

Life on the Selby Ranch was never boring and was often challenging, as with any family business that involves hundreds of cattle and other livestock and a dozen people working together to survive off the land. There were always financial challenges, injuries, strong differences of opinion on how to proceed in a situation, and so on. Nonetheless, four or five times every day Granny would simply stop whatever she was doing, go out onto the back porch, sit down in her rocking chair, let go of everything, and enjoy a few minutes of pure peace.

My first clear memories are of sitting in Granny's lap as she rocked on that porch, feeling absolutely safe and happy, immersed in her aura of acceptance and love. And throughout each day, she would help soothe people's upset feelings, bring renewed harmony to the household, and gently uplift everyone's spirits.

Although I never heard her speak these particular words, I feel that in her heart Granny was regularly saying to herself: "I choose to enjoy this moment."

As a child imitates its elders, I often encouraged people who were upset to feel better, and for this reason I was nicknamed "Buddy" when I was four. This, I suppose, is how a therapist is born. What amazes me in reflection is that, even in an extreme situation, Granny was able to maintain her ability to enjoy the present moment. Her son developed a fatal disease that slowly and painfully killed him; he lived out his final years in the family ranch house. And even as everyone else sank into a depressed sorrow while Uncle Jim withered away, Granny somehow still went out on the porch regularly, took a deep breath, tuned in to nature all around her, and shifted into a positive feeling in her heart.

What I learned from this example was that, even if our present moment seems terrible, we possess the power to reclaim positive feelings in our hearts. I remember Granny telling us one evening when Jim had fallen asleep that he was feeling bad enough as it was, without our pulling him down further by also feeling bad.

I now work with our local hospice and encourage the volunteer staff to approach dying patients with this same uplifting spirit. And whatever is happening around you, you can begin to explore your own power to say to yourself, "I choose to enjoy this moment," and see what happens.

*Every time you exercise*
*this particular mental and emotional muscle,*
*it will become stronger.*
*"I choose to enjoy this moment."*

## PLEASURE AS YOUR BIRTHRIGHT

Biologically, human beings tend to have the same basic pain-pleasure reflexes as other animals. We are programmed by our genes to contract away from pain and suffering, and to move toward pleasure and enjoyment. It's our nature to choose to enjoy each moment. This is how God made us. So how have we ended up focused overmuch on the agony of worrying, rather than focused on the pleasures of joyous living?

One of the main reasons is that human beings have the capacity to imagine all sorts of terrible things happening in the future, unlike other animals, who appear not to have this cognitive capacity. Whenever we're lost in future projections and worrying, we're not present in the here and now and, therefore, can't perceive, respond to, and effectively deal with any dangers that confront us.

In this light, worrying can be a dangerous act. When we're anxious, our minds and bodies tend to dysfunction. As a general rule, worrying makes us contract, become nervous and dizzy, think less clearly, and perform physically at a much lower level.

*When we think ourselves into a state of anxiety*
*we actually reduce our ability*
*to take care of ourselves*
*in the present moment.*

Another reason we spend so much time worrying is that, for countless generations, all over the world, power-fixated priests have used religion to program and manipulate people via fear-based beliefs. If we believe we're born sinners who will end up in eternal hellfire if we don't hop through a myriad of theological hoops, and if we accept that we must believe just the right things and never make our vengeful God angry, then how can we ever stop worrying about our religious doubts and simply ease up and enjoy the present moment?

*I humbly but fervently question*
*all religious theologies*
*that put the fear of the Lord,*
*rather than God's eternal love,*
*into children's hearts.*

As a former minister, I believe we're all created in God's perfect, loving image — we're essentially good by nature, not bad. I also believe it's our spiritual responsibility as well as our freedom to say no to worries, and focus on positive things most of the time, so that we bring more joy and love into the world, not more fear and contraction. What do you believe?

## MEDITATION AS REVOLUTION

Meditation enables us to quiet the attitudes and prejudices that our culture has programmed into us, and to distance ourselves from our fear-based beliefs and political inclinations. Leaders from time immemorial have known that a fearful population is easy to dominate. If meditation can free us from chronic manipulation by military, political, and economic powers, then meditation is indeed a revolutionary act against the fear-based status quo.

Meditation has traditionally been seen as a threat to Christianity because it encourages us to silence theological chatter about right and wrong, and to quiet our ego-based thoughts about religious beliefs, so that we can tune in to the direct spiritual experience of God's living presence in our lives. I remember thinking I was doing good as a young Presbyterian minister by teaching my youth group how to meditate. But I was unexpectedly called before a Holy Commission and kicked out of the Presbyterian community altogether, for experiencing and teaching the supposed heresy that we can know God's will and presence directly, beyond all human thoughts and writings.

*Because meditation, by its very nature,*
*incites freedom from established beliefs,*
*it is truly a revolutionary act that can threaten*
*dogmatic established orders.*

Revolution is usually spurred by an urgent need for change in the status quo. An honest look at our world situation indicates that a great deal of the violence in the world right now is caused by people of differing religious beliefs who judge and attack one another. Throughout history, opposing theological beliefs have generated hatred and violence.

A cure for this universal and tragic situation will occur when more people choose to regularly quiet their ingrained judgmental thoughts, through the process of meditation, and make a deeper connection with the divine. This meditative action enables us to tap directly into God's uplifting love, which we can then express in the world — that's a real revolution!

Krishnamurti often told us that there is a much-needed, universal revolution coming, one that must of necessity be a psychological revolution, transforming our inherited attitudes in a positive direction. He said:

> To bring about peace in the world,
> there must be a revolution in you and me.
> Economic revolution without this
> inward revolution is meaningless.
> To put an end to sorrow, to hunger, to war,
> there must be a psychological revolution.

To accomplish this psychological revolution, you must take charge of your own mind, quiet your fear-based thoughts, and focus more often each day on creative, loving, joyful actions. That's what you're learning to do here. I encourage you to hold the first Focus Phrase — "I choose to enjoy this moment" — often in your mind, as a peaceful revolutionary action that will help reduce fear and hostility in the world. When you tune in to joy in your own experience, you boost the overall love, acceptance, and harmony that we so deeply need right now.

> On close, honest observation,
> we see that people who are busy
> enjoying the present moment
> tend not to be harsh, in conflict, or violent —
> and so harmony prevails.

## SPIRITUAL EGO

The ego function of the mind is often labeled selfish and fearful, violent and power hungry — and therefore responsible for all our negative personality traits and, by extension, most of the world's woes. Meditative communities in particular often assume that the materialistic ego function must somehow be silenced, disengaged, or even killed, in order for us to progress spiritually.

*Ego* is a Greek term Sigmund Freud rebirthed a hundred years ago, referring to the power of our rational minds to use memories, attitudes, beliefs, concepts, future projections, and other cognitive activity to (1) gain a conceptual overview of a situation, (2) consider rational options, and (3) decide what's best for us to do in order to preserve our physical and emotional well-being.

So far, so good. We do need this cognitive function. But unfortunately the ego function often gets caught up in anxious imaginations and worries, as it tries to preserve and improve our mortal presence. Because it's responsible for future planning, a person's ego often becomes driven by apprehensions, and then tends to give in to greed and employ manipulation, aggression, and other spiritually negative thoughts and characteristics.

But wait — your ego is also the mental function that determines where you focus your attention from moment to moment. What a great power! Without the help of your ego as your personal inner guide, you will never focus your attention inward and master the meditation program I am offering you. Your ego is an essential player in the meditation game. So I encourage you to nurture your ego and respect its vital management role in your meditation experience, rather than trying to silence it or kill it off.

The good news is that you're already advancing beautifully toward this goal of integrating your ego function with your deeper spiritual advancement — because it's your ego that's focusing on reading this book. And each time you pause and move through one or more of the twelve Focus Phrases, it's your ego that decides to speak the Focus Phrases.

Except for when a deeper spiritual voice speaks to you, the voice you hear inside your own head is indeed your ego. And when you advance to where your ego voice and your spiritual voice become one, you will have reached a most beautiful state of consciousness.

I recommend that you pause, put this book aside for a few moments, and say the Focus Phrase "I choose to enjoy this moment" to yourself. Take time to reflect on who within you is the "I" that is choosing to redirect your attention to enjoying the present moment.

*Look deeply.*
*Let your mind be quiet.*
*Witness your own presence,*
*and open your heart and mind*
*to a new, insightful experience.*

*"I choose...to enjoy...this moment."*

## WORRIES — VALUABLE OR NOT?

Let's talk deeper into the notion of choosing to put worried thoughts permanently out of your mind. In teaching you this first Focus Phrase, I am suggesting that you stop aiming your attention in negative, fearful directions and instead focus on being positive and worry-free.

Most people believe that putting away all worries is a foolish thing to do. Our cultural assumption is that it's important for the ego to worry about dangers that might develop in the future, and to focus on avoiding those possible dangers. Won't we at some point get hit over the head by one of the real threats out there, if we stop worrying and just focus on feeling good in the present moment?

Ask yourself this: Is the process of worrying really advantageous, or does worrying interfere with our capacity to survive and enjoy life? As Krishnamurti often encouraged people to do, let's look at this question in the spirit of honest inquiry until we see the truth of the matter. I've already told you that, in my understanding, worrying about the future is utterly worthless, and that such ego worries impede our survival. Here's what my inquiry has found.

Human beings are considered more advanced than other mammals because we possess giant forebrains that amass loads of past experience (data) and then generate possible scenarios about what might happen in the future. Sometimes we create beautiful idealistic visions of the future. We also tend to generate negative, fear-based imaginations about terrible things that could happen to us or our loved ones — and then we spend a great deal of time trying to come up with strategies to avoid our imagined possibilities. This is a wise thing to do, yes?

No.

In cognitive therapy we've realized why Jesus, one of the truly enlightened psychologists, told us *not* to worry at all. His potent two-word dictum "Fear not!" is a clear command not to shift into fear mode — at all. Notice that Jesus didn't say, "Go into therapy and try to resolve all your anxieties." He said instead: "Don't go into fear mode — period."

As I mentioned earlier, when we shift into fear mode, a host of detrimental physiological, mental, and emotional reactions grip us and in turn seriously reduce our ability to think clearly, act with strength and endurance, and express valuable survival emotions such as empathy, confidence, team spirit, and spontaneity. Worrying is by definition counterproductive if we want to stay alert in the present moment and respond to situations appropriately.

You know that you shine at work and succeed in general when you're feeling positive, hopeful, and happy, and are tuned in to the pleasures of the present moment. And you tend to fail when you're anxious, depressed, lost in worries about the future, or feeling guilty and remorseful about the past. To see this clearly is to educate your ego to recognize that saying, "I choose to enjoy this moment," is the wise action, not just for spiritual well-being but also for biological survival.

Of course, when you're in a dangerous situation, you do need to focus on the danger and deal with it. Face your danger! But don't stay chronically fixated on fearful imaginations about the future. Instead, exercise your freedom to take charge of your mind, use cognitive tools that help you break free from the worry trip — enjoy your life rather than wasting it in anxious contraction.

We all struggle with worrying, and I'm not saying it's easy to stop feeling anxious. I'm just suggesting that you begin right now to commit yourself to learning how to regularly shift your focus of attention from worry to its opposite — full, confident participation in the unfolding moment. Krishnamurti put it this way: "If your eyes are blinded with your worries, you cannot see the beauty of the sunset."

## MAKE A JOYFUL NOISE

If your purpose in life isn't to worry all the time, nor to attempt to second-guess fate and avoid life's problems, then what is your purpose? My own understanding of this question first came during a radical gathering of spiritually minded folk way back in the early seventies. I'd chosen to go into the ministry to serve my country spiritually rather than go to Vietnam as a soldier — and I chose to go to the most radical seminary I could find, which at the time was the San Francisco Theological Seminary, just north of the city.

Those were wild spiritual times, to put it mildly, and I'm thankful to have been at that seminary for four formative years — even though, after I graduated from seminary, I was summarily kicked out of the Presbyterian Church for being too much in the Buddhist and Hindu camps and not enough on the side of John Calvin and the Puritans.

I remember reading during my seminary days this quote from the Chinese sage Lao-tzu:

> *I do not concern myself*
> *with gods and spirits*
> *either good or evil,*
> *nor do I serve any.*

And Krishnamurti weighed in with this succinct statement about remaining a free thinker:

> *The following of authority*
> *is the denial of intelligence.*
> *In the process, self-knowledge*
> *and freedom are abandoned.*

In the spirit of honest inquiry, my seminary often hosted open spiritual discussions, one of which is related to our current "choose to enjoy this moment" theme and still rings clear in my mind. Let me take you back to that evening up on Holy

Hill, where about fifty students came to meet with four of our community's deeper spiritual teachers, to discuss Christian, Jewish, Hindu, and Buddhist approaches to sin, guilt, pleasure, contemplation, and humankind's responsibility (if any) to God the Creator.

After an hour or so of open discussion, someone asked the four leaders if they'd finish by sharing what was most important to them right then regarding their responsibility to God.

Professor Mylenberg, a convert from Jewish academia who was pushing eighty and dying of brain cancer, a truly wise human being, spoke up first. He told us of losing his parents, aunt, and sister at Auschwitz, and of somehow surviving by going into an inner world where he shut out everything negative and chanted, "Make a joyful noise unto the Lord, all ye lands," over and over to himself, until he began to hear only that joyful noise and nothing else.

"God doesn't even need us to be in tune," I remember him saying with tears in his eyes. "It can just be noise — but it must be joyful. Our spiritual responsibility is to hold that positive light of God brightly in our hearts."

Werner Eisenach, another remarkable professor at the seminary, had been an officer in the German army and then imprisoned and tortured for speaking about his anti-Hitler persuasions. He talked to us about his months in solitary confinement, where a biblical passage had haunted him and transformed his life — Jesus's commandment "Be ye therefore perfect, even as your Father in heaven is perfect."

Werner told us that suddenly one night, when he was feeling utterly depressed, his mind had exploded with the realization that, even in his miserable situation, he was indeed God's perfect creation. How could he be less than perfect if he was made in God's image? And if each new moment was a creation of God's, then each moment, no matter how ugly it seemed, must also be perfect. This realization pushed him into a state of inner bliss that lasted for weeks.

The third person on the informal panel that night was a British former minister and current Zen hedonist, as he defined himself, the philosopher Alan Watts, with whom I'd become quite close in the preceding two years. He'd spent a number of years at a Zen monastery in Japan before returning to San Francisco as a renegade father figure of the psychedelic revolution. Often at gatherings he was full of humor, but that night he was somber.

He said that long ago he'd let go of any childhood imaginations of a personal God to whom he was in any way responsible. For him, his spiritual responsibility was to regularly quiet the mind, free it of all thoughts, enter into silence, and tap directly into the spontaneous guidance and joy that was always waiting to rise up in the center of one's being.

After a short silence, the fourth member of the panel, an elderly man named Sam Lewis, better known as Sufi Sam, began talking. Highly respected as a great teacher not limited to any specific theology or dogma, he smiled warmly at us, said a few words of greeting, and then sat quietly for about five minutes. Then suddenly he reopened his eyes and told us upfront that he was the eyes and ears of God — his primary purpose was simply to be aware, to stay here in the present moment and not get lost in thoughts about the past or the future.

He then asked us: "Are you also the eyes and ears of God? Right now, is God here because he's experiencing this moment through our awareness? And when we're gone from the present moment, lost in thought, are we denying God this moment?"

Somehow I knew deep down that what he'd said was true. Ever since, when I find myself lost in problem solving, fantasies about the future, memories, and the chronic stream of thought that pulls me away from the present moment, I feel that I'm shutting God off from enjoying this moment with me — and my attention pops back into the eternal present.

Don't get me wrong — I love to think, and there's definitely a place in each day for all the different phases of consciousness. Mostly we spend our days in action mode, doing this and thinking that, planning for the future and reflecting on the past. Fine. But we also need regular "being breaks" when we quiet our thoughts and return to the experience of being one with God (by whatever name we call God) so that our experience is God's experience.

Osho spoke of "witnessing," by which he meant alertly experiencing what's happening around us and within us, without judging or manipulating what's happening — simply witnessing reality:

> *You are an observer.*
> *Whatever is happening*
> *just be a witness.*
> *This is your authentic nature.*
> *No judgment, no evaluation,*
> *no condemnation, no appreciation —*
> *just pure observing.*
>
> *Out of this witnessing*
> *a great awareness arises*
> *bringing compassion, love, bliss.*

## WHAT TO DO

You are now perhaps beginning to sense the value of the first Focus Phrase. It has clear reverberating power when said on its own. It also has special power when used as the beginning of the full twelve-step Uplift process. For now, let's consider it alone. I described at the beginning of this chapter one way in which I've used the first Focus Phrase in action. Wherever you are, you can bring to mind the words "I choose to enjoy this moment," and they will help shift your attention to your ongoing internal and external positive experiences at that moment.

## MEDITATION IN ACTION

We've seen how the first Focus Phrase can help you let go of worrying. It will equally help you let go of hostile fixations, depressive thoughts, guilt, shame, and all other negative mental habits that tend to pull you down and prevent you from enjoying the present.

The next time you're in a long line at the checkout stand of a store, or stuck in traffic, or waiting for an appointment, or out walking, or listening to a discussion at work, or somewhere else, notice whether you're enjoying the moment or either torturing yourself with negative thoughts and emotions or just lost in rambling thoughts. Right at that moment, decide to shift your attention to enjoying the present moment. Bring to mind the Focus Phrase "I choose to enjoy this moment," and set yourself free.

That's called meditation in action, and it's one of the most important dimensions of meditation. Not only will you transform your inner experience, but you'll also radiate good feelings and harmony to those around you. You'll become an active, positive force in your world.

## MEDITATION AT WORK

It's relatively easy to retreat to a mountaintop and focus on enjoying the present moment. It's an entirely different situation when you immerse yourself in the inherent stress and conflict of the workplace. That's why it's so important to arm yourself each morning with cognitive tools that help you hold on to the joy of life, even at work.

I encourage you to develop a new habit at work — at least once in the morning and once in the afternoon, pause for just a short time (even four breaths will do) and say one or more Focus Phrases to yourself. You need not make any effort beyond just remembering to say the elicitor statements. The seeming magic of these Focus Phrases is that the simple act of bringing them to mind and saying them silently to yourself makes something happen.

By choosing to enjoy each moment regardless of what's happening around you, you not only reduce your own stress and upset feelings on the job but also boost the spirit of your entire workplace. You uplift the world around you by choosing consciously to enjoy each new moment.

At lunch or during a break, see if you can again bring to mind Focus Phrases that redirect your attention in directions that you value. Each new chapter of this book discusses in depth a new Focus Phrase that will carry great power in your life, if you let it. You'll find that often, during a lunch break, a particular Focus Phrase will dominate your awareness because it relates to what's happening at work. Hold this Focus Phrase in the back of your mind as you reenter the work fray, so that you maintain a bright state of consciousness throughout the day. This will promote both your personal success and the well-being of those you work with.

## MEDITATION AT HOME

When I get up in the morning, I routinely make a cup of tea and then sit for five minutes or so in a comfortable easy chair in the living room, quiet and alone. All I do is sit down and say to myself, "I choose to enjoy this moment," and breathe pure beingness for a few minutes.

Often I also move through the full set of twelve Focus Phrases for a complete realignment of my mind and soul in directions that I find rewarding and healing. But just saying the first Focus Phrase, and then breathing the experience that the words elicit, is a wonderful way to start the day.

When you come home from work, you can use one or more Focus Phrases to defuse tensions and emotions you picked up at work. Hold in mind that the Focus Phrases are both spiritual tools and psychological tools — there's really no separating the two. You can't enter into a spiritual, meditative state of consciousness until you first defuse the psychological disturbances that grip you.

In later chapters we'll explore the inherent logic found in the linear order of the twelve Focus Phrases. As a unit, they constitute a clear progression away from all that bothers you emotionally and mentally, toward the deeper spiritual joy that emerges naturally when you quiet your mental chatter and emotional turbulence. I have given you the first tool. Apply it often; choose to focus on good feelings in the here and now.

Finally, you come to the end of your day. This is probably the optimum time to set aside a longer period for deep meditation, if you so choose.

All you have to do is sit down and give yourself free time to just be. "Nowhere to go, nothing to do," as the Zen folk say.

Get comfortable...let the dust settle...and then allow the first Focus Phrase to come to mind. Say it to yourself as you exhale: "I choose to enjoy this moment."

Without effort, as you hold these potent elicitor words in your mind, allow them to do their magic in refocusing your attention on your breathing and your simple beingness, right here, right now. And be open to an always-new quiet-mind experience!

*I choose...to enjoy...this moment.*

CHAPTER TWO

# REFRESH YOUR BREATH LINK

*The solar plexus is the point*
*at which the part meets with the whole,*
*where the Infinite becomes finite,*
*Universal becomes individualized,*
*Invisible becomes visible.*

*It is the point at which life appears —*
*and there is no limit to the amount of life*
*you can generate from this solar center.*

— CHARLES HAANEL

Long before I started kindergarten, I was a natural student of another teacher who influenced me greatly, in addition to my grandmother — my grandfather John Selby, from whom I also got my name. He was an old-time rancher in the Ojai Valley, over the hill from Santa Barbara. Long before the term *horse whisperer* was in vogue, he was known as the master horse trainer in our region.

One of Gramps's main techniques for successfully gaining the trust of a horse just happens to also be the primary beginning technique of most meditation programs. "I just tune in to the rhythm that the horse's breath is caught up in at the moment," he explained to me one day. "If I'm tuned in to my own breathing and the breathing of the horse at the same time, something pretty magical seems to happen. I stop thinking about what I want to do with the horse and instead just focus on our breaths coming and going, and pretty soon I'm breathing along with him. We both calm down and pay attention to each other. Then the rest is mostly easy."

I didn't pay much attention to this explanation at the time, being so young. Then a dozen years later, what Gramps had said to me resurfaced when I received my first formal meditation training during my freshman year at Princeton, from a very fine teacher from China who taught the school's comparative religions course.

He was a lay Buddhist meditator, and on Thursday evenings he led a casual meditation class for interested students. He talked a bit about the goals of meditation, and then asked us to just sit comfortably and do our best to pay full attention to the air flowing in and out of our noses for the next half hour.

I remembered my grandfather and smiled to myself. Then I tried to do as instructed, but very quickly found the challenge almost impossible. You've probably had this experience as well. For perhaps three or four breaths, it's relatively easy to focus on your breathing. But very quickly your thinking mind pushes its way to the fore again, and your breath awareness drops away.

For my grandfather, the challenge was much easier because he wasn't just sitting quietly and watching his breathing. His whole body was actively engaged in gentle movements as he walked around the horse. In other words, he was entirely absorbed in the sensory perceptual world within and around him. Many great athletes speak of the same state of mind when they talk about being "in the zone" while performing whole-body actions.

For years while in formal meditation in the Hindu and Buddhist traditions, I struggled along with everyone else to quiet my thinking mind and tune in to my breathing for longer periods of time. There is, of course, much to be gained in this meditative struggle, and certain people succeed and move forward with traditional meditation. But most people fail and then drop out of meditation right at this beginning point.

Here's a typical instruction for Vipassana meditation that I found on the website of a Buddhist meditation center:

*Assume the sitting meditation body posture*
*and gaze straight ahead without blinking or shifting.*
*With lucid and non-conceptual mindfulness,*
*you should keep your attention vividly present*
*and stay focused on the breaths coming and going.*

*In this quiet state look into the mind itself*
*to see what shape, color and other qualities it has.*
*Remain detached throughout.*

*Continue watching your breathing*
*and watching your mind*
*until the end of the meditation.*

I'm not going to assign you this traditional Buddhist challenge. Instead I'd like to show you a new psychological understanding of breath awareness that will make this whole beginning process both easy and enjoyable.

## EXPERIENCE VERSUS REFLECTION

First of all, let's get clear on some basic rules concerning how your mind works. There are two primary modes of consciousness — you are either focused primarily on the present moment and processing direct perceptual sensory information or

focused on the memory of a perceptual experience as you reflect on that experience through symbolic cognition.

You'll find that it's this interplay between experiencing and
reflecting on experience that occupies most of your waking moments. Raw sensory experience is the perceptual foundation of
everything you think and imagine.

When you're reflecting on an experience, you're focusing
your attention on the past, on memories of your sensory and
emotional experience that you've stored. Analytical reflective
thinking is just that — an analysis of a past memory, generating
conceptual thought, expanded concepts, imaginations, and plans.

When you're busy thinking, you mostly let go of present-
moment sensory experience in order to focus on your thoughts
about a past event, or imagination, about the future. It's important to realize that, when you drift into thought, you are actually losing contact with the experiential present moment.

*Meditation is the conscious act*
*of shifting out of past-future thinking*
*and returning your awareness*
*to the present moment —*
*which is where*
*you live your life.*

People often think that meditation is a process of going
away from the world. My understanding of true meditation is
that, through it, people become more fully alive and involved
in the world. Abstract thought is a wonderful tool. But we do
need to put that tool aside regularly if we want to engage with
and influence the emerging reality of our lives.

A healthy balance between experience and reflection usually

leads to a healthy personality. Most neuroses and psychoses involve a distorted fixation with thoughts, memories, fantasies, and forebodings. You actively reduce your neurotic tendencies by becoming more aware of your breathing. As you purposefully shift your attention away from the thoughts and imaginations that make you feel upset or afraid, you nurture a healthy inner life and more fully engage with the world around you.

When you're skiing down a hill, running through the forest, making love, cooking in the kitchen, or doing some other whole-body action, you will find that being in the zone and staying aware of your breathing are relatively easy. But when you are sitting quietly and doing nothing physically, the thinking mind almost always takes over from the perceptual mind and dominates the show.

In a traditional meditative practice, your teacher would probably insist that you must dig in and discipline yourself for months and perhaps years to quiet your thinking mind. Although it's interesting to watch one's own thoughts and observe one's own habitual mental patterns, I personally have never found anything holy in fixating overlong on this inner battle to silence the chronic flow of thoughts.

Pragmatically, it seems wise to quiet the mind in as efficient a manner as possible. This is why I've applied new insights in cognitive and perceptual psychology to the "battle of the mind" and put the battle aside once and for all.

## FOCUS PHRASES TO THE RESCUE

As I mentioned in passing earlier, rather than trying to force the thinking mind to shut up, it's much better to give the thinking mind something valuable to do in the meditation process. Focus Phrases serve that purpose beautifully. While you're holding a Focus Phrase in mind, all other thoughts naturally become quiet. You keep your thinking mind busy thinking specific words that focus it away from thinking.

For me, this is using spiritual judo (going with the flow) rather than karate (fighting against the flow) to quiet the mind. Rather than telling your ego to go off in the far corner and shut up, you respectfully give it something genuinely important to do during the meditative process. As you explore this book, it will be your ego that remembers to say the Focus Phrases that shift your attention, and this remembering is essential to success. Psychologically, the ego needs to be included and welcomed as a key player in the spiritual game.

Notice for yourself what happens when you say the Focus Phrase of this chapter:

*I feel the air flowing in and out of my nose.*

As you experiment with it, you'll experience how the very act of saying these words to yourself effortlessly stimulates a shift in your attention toward the physical sensation of the air as it flows in and out of your nose. In the process, as you shift into perception mode, your regular thoughts will naturally become quiet. Thoughts don't always have to lead to other thoughts. They also have the power to refocus your attention on experiencing. This is a valuable clue to how we can optimally manage our own minds.

Again, say to yourself the second focus phrase, "I feel the air flowing in and out of my nose." Notice that you are not telling yourself to *think about* your breathing, but telling yourself to tune in to the *feeling* of your breath experience — the physical sensations being stimulated as millions of air molecules rush past the sensitive follicles in your nose.

Each word in a Focus Phrase carries considerable power — these are called elicitor terms because they provoke action in your mind. The first Focus Phrase, "I choose to enjoy this moment," elicits action as you shift your attention to enjoyable present-moment experiences. It's the same with "I feel the air flowing in and out of my nose" and equally with the other ten Focus Phrases you'll be learning — they provoke a shift in attention in directions that will serve you powerfully.

When you say a series of Focus Phrases in order, they lead you step-by-step through the chosen process. This is the full meditative potential we're aiming at. But you can also take just one focus phrase and say it over and over again to yourself, to fill your mind with its elicitor words. This is a powerful way to override the habitual mental chatter that usually dominates your mind, as well as a way to induce a valuable experience related to that Focus Phrase.

This is especially true of the phrase "I feel the air flowing in and out of my nose." The sooner you can make this a habitual mantra in the back of your mind, the quicker this entire meditative process will provoke transformation in your life. Try it:

*I feel the air flowing in and out of my nose.*

## WHY FOCUS ON BREATHING?

This is a good question. After all, what's so important about breathing? Isn't watching one's breathing boring? From our very first moments of life outside our mother's womb, we've been breathing nonstop. And we're going to continue breathing right up until our last moment alive. How can something so mundane as breathing be such an important spiritual event? And in particular, what's so holy about focusing on one's nose?

There are several different ways to answer this question, each of them important. First of all, consider this: Thinking happens inside your own skull. Physically, the location of your cognitive activity is in the head. So when you're lost in thought, your focus is up high, in your cranium, deep inside your neurological brain. The purpose of the first phase of meditation is to shift your awareness beyond the cognitive function of your brain toward your whole-body presence in the eternal present moment.

Notice how close your nose is to your brain — very close indeed. Breathing through your nose is a constant sensory event, and it is happening near your thinking center. So it makes perfect sense to focus, during the first expansion of consciousness, a short distance from where your thoughts are taking place, on a sensory event that's always happening and therefore always available to tune in to. I suspect this is why breath awareness in the nose has become the most universal meditative practice.

Beyond this obvious physiological reason is the fact that breath is life. The Judeo-Christian Bible states that God breathed life into man. This dramatic statement implies that God has breath, and that it is God's breath that fills us with life moment by moment.

*If you stop breathing for five minutes, you're dead.*
*Breath is life.*
*And so, to focus on breathing is*
*to focus on a core element*
*of your earthly existence.*

This is surely another major reason that a primary aspect of all meditation traditions is breath awareness. There's also a third key reason for beginning meditation with a focus on the nose and breath awareness: in actual practice, most people are unable to enter into the later steps of meditation unless they first focus on their breathing. Early on, when doing what is called pranayana breath meditation, I found that the meditation worked for me only when I first focused on the breath in my nose, then expanded my focus to include my breathing in my chest and belly, and then expanded to include my whole body.

The wake-up experience I described in the introduction reinforced this progression — unless I begin by focusing on the air flowing in and out of my nose, I find it very difficult to move to the next steps in the expansion process. We can't yet prove scientifically that, in general, consciousness expansion requires the beginner to focus breath awareness on the nose, but in actual practice this seems the most effective beginning point.

Krishnamurti offers this simple breath challenge: "Can you with one breath, with one look, know yourself very simply as you are?"

## YOUR NOSE KNOWS

I am often asked what is the proper way to focus on the experience of air flowing in and out of the nose. The answer is simple: there is no proper way. There is no predictable experience. The magic thing about the present moment is that it never repeats itself.

By definition, at any given moment the universe is in a unique situation: what is happening will never repeat itself. In this physical universe, time does march on. You can never have the same experience twice.

Please take this scientific fact to heart. So many people fail at meditation because they have an amazing experience and then try to duplicate it the next time they meditate. In doing so, they slip further and further into memory and imagination and submerge themselves in a comfortable inner experience — but one based mostly on the repetition of a memory or on imagination; it is not a new spiritual encounter. This is called spiritual masturbation — it can feel good, yes, but it prevents true engagement with the emerging spiritual moment.

When you focus your attention on the air flowing in and out of your nose right now, realize that the experience you are having has never happened before and will never happen again. That is the remarkable power of meditative consciousness — it's always new! Whenever you focus on the air flowing in and out of your nose, it's important to put aside all memories of other breath experiences, put aside all imaginations about breathing, and simply experience the pure, unique perceptual event happening right now. When you do this, you open a door, via your breathing, to the entire universe of experience happening right now within and around you.

*Breath awareness is the spiritual portal*
*into the eternal moment.*
*Your nose knows.*

## I CHALLENGE YOU

One of my favorite people of all time was Humphrey Osmond, a psychiatrist who, at the time I knew him, ran the New Jersey Neuro-Psychiatric Institute's Bureau of Research in Neurology and Psychiatry. Humphrey was a schizophrenic who had surrendered to, accepted, and conquered schizophrenia, and was devoting his life to studying the polar dynamics of mental illness and mystic experience. I did my first research under his guidance. As a loving friend and my first training therapist, he helped me through some pretty radical times in my early twenties.

I had a series of weekly therapy sessions with Humphrey as part of my training, and the first thing he said to me when we started was that he wanted to pose a challenge. He challenged me to stay aware of my own breathing regardless of whatever else happened during our therapy sessions — and to make everything else secondary.

Usually people think they can't be aware of their breathing and do other things at the same time. It's true that we often lose awareness of our breathing when we're busy at work or lost in thought. Humphrey was challenging me to enter a more expanded, integrative awareness where the intuitive function of the mind becomes active, generating thoughts beyond those of the everyday thinking mind.

*We usually do our best work*
*when we remain aware*
*of our breathing.*

Ask great basketball players if they're tuned in to their breathing when they're out on the court. Of course they are. Successful performance is a whole-body present-moment action. And when we expand our awareness to include our breathing, we're able to function in the zone more often.

In this spirit, I'm sitting here "talking" this book into existence and staying aware of my breathing while doing so. Each day of my life, I continue to do my best to fulfill Humphrey's challenge. And I challenge you to do the same.

## BREATH FOREMOST

Let's begin the challenge right now. As you read through the rest of this chapter and the rest of this book, stay aware of the air flowing in and out of your nose during each new breath.

Notice how easy it is to read what I'm saying and at the same time experience the breathing sensations in your nose. This is the first step in the expansion of consciousness. You're learning to expand your awareness, and maintain that expanded state of consciousness.

The air flowing in . . . the air flowing out . . .

Also notice that you don't have to make any effort to breathe — ever. Breathing happens all on its own. You can definitely inhibit your natural breathing by generating particular negative emotions. I'm sure you know what anxiety does to your breathing: it becomes tight and shallow, high up in the chest, reducing your oxygen intake and making you dizzy and mentally dysfunctional. And if you get caught up in depressive memories or expectations, your breathing will become slow and lethargic and reduce your oxygen intake.

When left to itself, your breathing will almost always beautifully match your oxygen needs, expanding and speeding up when you move, slowing its pace and reducing its depth when you slow down.

Notice your breathing as it continues right now in its natural in-and-out pulsation. Make absolutely no effort to inhale or exhale — set your breathing free. Let your breathing stop when it wants to . . . and begin again when it wants to, all on its own.

Sometimes your breathing will pause at the top of your

inhalation, or pause when you're empty of air at the bottom of your exhalation — or anywhere in between. And when you set your breathing entirely free to do whatever it wants, you'll find that it naturally begins to smooth out and deepen. This feels very good.

When you're unconscious of your breathing, you can fall victim to all sorts of negative tension and unpleasant feelings. But as soon as you shine the light of your awareness on your breathing, you begin to self-correct. Every time you remember to say, "I feel the air flowing in and out of my nose," your breathing will spontaneously begin to recover from whatever emotional tension might be impeding it.

The healing process in general is intimately related to your habitual breathing experience, and increased breath awareness is one of the most powerful ways to stimulate physical and emotional healing. I used to teach all sorts of complex self-healing programs, but these days I mostly just assist people in regularly redirecting their attention to their breathing, so that their inhalations and exhalations relax, deepen, and shift into a healthier, more natural rhythm. This in turn activates the organic healing process that happens on its own when the breathing is free.

If you regularly do the following, you will be well on the way to activating your own healing process at whatever level you need:

1.  Give yourself permission to feel good in the present moment.
2.  Turn your loving attention to your breathing.
3.  Allow your breathing to relax and expand and regain its natural rhythm.

We'll speak more of this in later chapters.

## REMEMBER THE CHALLENGE

Uhm...I don't mean to be a bother, but are you still aware of your breathing? Are you allowing your breaths to come and go without effort? Are you giving yourself permission to enjoy the experience? And are you holding in the back of your mind the secular breathing mantra "I feel the air flowing in and out of my nose?"

As you tune in to the experience of air flowing in and out of your nose, you naturally shift your center of awareness to that interior nasal location in your physical body. Especially as you inhale, you might have a sharp feeling in your nose. The air flowing in will be the temperature of the air around you, which is usually cooler than your body temperature, creating stimulation in the nose. The lungs heat the air, so when you exhale through your nose there is less sensation. For the same reason, you perceive scents more strongly as you inhale than as you exhale.

> *I've reached the point in my life*
> *where I feel that I'm not fully*
> *here in the world as a living organism*
> *when I'm not aware of the air flowing*
> *in and out of my nose.*
> *Some dimension is definitely missing*
> *when I get lost in thought.*

As I'll discuss, cognitive thought is a two-dimensional function of the mind, whereas perceptual experience is a three-dimensional experience. Deductive thinking is by definition a past-future symbolic process that has no depth — the words moving through your mind don't have volume. They exist in a flat, two-dimensional zone of the mind.

But when you shift from deductive thinking to sensory experience, you resume three-dimensional existence. Every time you switch from being lost in thought to focusing on the sensations stimulated by the air flowing in and out of your nose, your consciousness expands from two dimensions to three. This is a gigantic leap: you shift from being not fully present to being fully immersed in the sensory world.

And once you fully engage with the world, something truly marvelous is enabled in you. You become capable of thinking creative, intuitive thoughts as you tap into the higher integrated functions of the mind, where experience, thought, and spirit cocreate.

With this second Focus Phrase, you now have a powerful tool. I encourage you to say to yourself, "I feel the air flowing in and out of my nose," over and over during the next hours, days, and weeks, so that you program your mind with this driving intent to put breath awareness first in your life and everything else second.

Your life will become more vital and enjoyable as a result. I'm sometimes criticized for being too simplistic at this level of my teachings, but sometimes the simplest is the most powerful. Don't take my word for this. Instead, as you read these words, feel the air flowing in and out of your nose. Notice for yourself how each moment you spend in an expanded breath-conscious state is a moment in which you seem fully alive.

Throughout this book I'll remind you that Spirit inflows only in the present moment, when you're in sensory, here-and-now mode. And the most direct way to shift into the here and now is to hold the following statement of intent in your mind:

*I feel the air flowing in and out of my nose.*

## ANCHORING

One of the best ways to actively bring the Focus Phrases into your life is to "anchor" them, by linking a particular Focus Phrase to a particular situation in your daily routine. For instance, in a program that teaches Focus Phrases to hospital nurses in order to reduce accidents, nurses learn to anchor a Focus Phrase to a particular visual or movement situation they regularly encounter at work.

You can do the same in your own life. Let's begin with the first Focus Phrase. Here's an example of what I do. As I mentioned earlier, when I wake up I usually make a cup of tea and sit in my easy chair in the living room for a few minutes or more of quiet meditation. As soon as I sit in my chair (my anchor), I remember to say the first Focus Phrase: "I choose to enjoy this moment."

Because I've anchored that Focus Phrase in my morning routine, I quickly shift to feeling bright and good every morning, able to aim my attention exactly where I choose. This way I don't fall victim to chronic thoughts and emotions that might otherwise grab my attention.

After breakfast at home, here in Hawaii, I usually walk a few minutes through a small forest to my office and studio. Five to ten times a day, I walk back and forth between my home and work space. And as soon as I start out across the back lawn, or out of my studio and into the forest to go home, I say the second Focus Phrase, which I've anchored to that particular situation. Out of habit, I say, "I feel the air flowing in and out of my nose," and immediately all the buzz, all thought of past and future related to my work space, is put aside, and I tune in to the pure pleasure of the present moment. Find similar anchors for yourself and, in this simple way, you'll enjoy a minivacation several times a day. This is a pure blessing.

So many people push themselves nonstop throughout each day, planning to someday retire and not work at all. My advice is to instead find minivacations many times each day, using the Zen Awakening part of the Focus Phrase program to instantly shift you into inner paradise.

I've established other anchor points in my daily routine as well. Whenever I check my email, I pause and see what Focus Phrase comes to mind, and for the next three or four breaths I allow it to positively affect me. And when I get into my car, before I turn the ignition key, I allow a Focus Phrase to come to mind for three or four breaths before firing up my auto. When making love, I pause and say the first few Focus Phrases to myself in order to shift fully into present-moment, whole-body presence. Before eating, I pause for a Focus Phrase moment. I do the same in the shower.

Unless I'm on the road, I usually return to my easy chair in the evening to read for an hour or two, and as I sit down I move through the full set of twelve Focus Phrases. Then, in bed before going to sleep, I almost always see what Focus Phrase comes to mind and, in that relaxed state of consciousness, open up to an expanded experience.

Here's a list of my ten primary Focus Phrase anchors, which I enjoyably honor and employ each day when I'm home. (I have a somewhat different list for when I'm traveling.)

Morning tea
　Walk to work
　　Walk to house
　　　Before checking email
　　　　Before starting the car
　　　　　Making love
　　　　　　Before eating
　　　　When showering
　　　Evening easy chair
　Just before sleep

I challenge you to identify and write down five to ten often-repeated situations in your own daily routine. Begin to anchor the Focus Phrase process to these visual, cognitive, or movement-related situations. This is perhaps the most important responsibility that you'll take on as you master these Focus Phrases. Give yourself as many minivacations each day as you want — they're entirely free, they don't disrupt your routine, they recharge your inner batteries, and they allow Spirit to regularly flow into your life.

To end this chapter, I recommend that you pause for a few moments, tune in to your breathing, and see what daily routines pop into your mind that you might readily anchor to a momentary Focus Phrase experience. Start to write your anchor list — it's important to make a list. And right away, begin attaching Focus Phrases to these anchor points. You already know the first two phrases, and soon you'll have the whole set of twelve.

*I choose to enjoy this moment.*
*I feel the air flowing in and out of my nose.*

CHAPTER THREE

# WAKE UP YOUR SOLAR PLEXUS

*The process of meditation*
*does not take you to a new world.*
*The process of meditation*
*does not add anything to you.*

*Meditation means an alertness*
*a freshness, a constant wakefulness.*
*To meditate means to be aware*
*of the whole process of life.*

*Sit on the bank*
*of the stream of the mind*
*where there is no thought.*
*There is meditation.*

—— OSHO

You've now learned two Focus Phrases that pack serious power and can transform your daily experience. The second Focus Phrase helps you shift your attention to your nose. In traditional Hindu meditation, this is the area of the sixth chakra or energy center, associated with higher intuitive thinking and spiritual realization. The third Focus Phrase, introduced in this chapter, will expand your awareness to include both your head and your full torso, so that you focus attention on all seven energy centers of your body.

Experientially, there is no separating your spiritual awareness from your bodily awareness, because your awareness emerges within your bodily presence. As Alan Watts so aptly put it: "What we are is first of all the whole of our body."

In my early twenties I was introduced to chakra meditation by a young man named Kriyananda, one of the main disciples of the Hindu master Yogananda. While devoutly practicing his kriyayoga chakra meditations, I was amazed to discover from the inside that indeed we do have seven distinct energy centers located in the head and torso. These chakras exist not only as lofty religious concepts but also as definite energetic phenomena that can be readily experienced during meditation. While moving through the first steps of the meditation process I'm teaching you, you'll naturally become more aware of these energy centers.

For four years, I explored the classic yoga techniques for encountering and manipulating my seven chakras. In kundalini meditation, it's possible to generate the most remarkable sensations of internal energy flow imaginable. A disciple studies and internalizes a complex conceptual model of how the chakras interact with one another, and how kundalini energy can be manipulated to flow through the chakra system. Then the disciple attempts to duplicate the internal energetic process the master has described.

While studying at Princeton, however, I'd worked as a hypnotic subject in research with Dr. Bernard Aaronson at the National Institutes of Health, and Dr. Aaronson could use hypnosis to elicit all sorts of fantasy energy events. So I knew the amazing power of the mind to produce a vivid inner experience based on imagination, not real sensory stimulation.

In my kundalini training with Kriyananda, I began to suspect that my amazing experiences of energy flowing up and down my spine were being generated mostly by my imagination, not by any spiritual or perceptual reality. I also realized that spending so much time trying to stimulate a spiritual thrill wasn't what I wanted to do with my life. I was giving myself great pleasure, but in the process was disengaging from the world. I learned a great deal from Hindu studies and meditation, but my larger goal was to understand the psychological underpinnings of meditation, so I decided to explore other methods.

Looking back, I can see that I went a bit overboard. Not only did I stop trying to manipulate my chakras but I also stopped focusing on my seven energy centers during meditation.

Ten years later, while working in West Berlin, I met and had deep conversations with the remarkable and often misunderstood renegade guru Osho, then called Bhagwan Rajneesh, whose spiritual writings still inspire new generations. Osho helped to reawaken my interest in the natural organic presence of the seven chakras in my own body, and showed me a new way to relate to these energy centers.

I remember Osho laughing at me in his good-natured way when I told him my negative opinion of chakra meditation. His advice was that I again take time daily to aim my attention at each of the chakra centers in my body, but that I do it this time without indulging in any conceptual imagination of what I might find.

"Please look! Only look!" he said emphatically.

I took his advice, and I give you the same: throw away all your preconceptions, if you have any, and simply become more aware of what you find when you look inward with a quiet, receptive mind.

In this spirit, let's take a closer look at what's traditionally considered the lower chakras, located in the torso — especially the breath chakra in and around your solar plexus and diaphragm muscle.

## EXPANDING YOUR BUBBLE

We each live in a unique bubble of personal awareness that is, experientially, the full extent of our individual life on this planet. What delineates our experience from moment to moment is the fact that our awareness bubble is constantly contracting or expanding. We're either more aware, or less aware — and our total life experience depends, ultimately, on how expansive or contracted our bubble of awareness has been during our lives.

Most people seem to live most of the time mostly in their heads — their awareness bubble is small and fixed on the ego's chronic thoughts about the past and the future. And because cognitive thought doesn't seem to have the dimension of volume, our awareness bubble presents a two-dimensional world.

Meditation is about purposefully expanding your bubble of awareness to include your whole being, and the living world around you. When you say to yourself, "I choose to enjoy this moment," you expand your bubble beyond the thoughts in your head, so that you're aware of your body in the present moment. That's a major expansion. Likewise, when you say to yourself, "I feel the air flowing in and out of my nose," you're choosing to expand your bubble beyond your mind's mental activities into the seemingly infinite sensory universe.

With the third Focus Phrase, "I also feel the movements in my chest and belly as I breathe," your bubble of awareness naturally expands to include not just your nose and head but also your chest, belly, and pelvis. As you activate this new Focus Phrase, you'll find that you experience a heightened sense of space and volume in your body and a three-dimensional awareness of your life-sustaining lungs and heart.

Let me guide you through this process. Always begin with the first Focus Phrase: "I choose to enjoy this moment." This statement of positive intent will make sure that, as you focus on your breathing, you choose to enjoy the experience of focusing on your breathing. With a little practice you'll find that, even as you say the first Focus Phrase, your attention will naturally expand to include your breath experience.

Your breathing is intimately involved in the process of feeling joy and pleasure in your body. There's actually no way to separate your emotional feelings and your breath experience; they're neurologically one and the same. An emotion is a whole-body sensory response that includes your breathing as an intricate and essential part of the emotion itself. So as you tune in to your breathing, you tune in to your emotions. If you're anxious or depressed or angry, you will express these emotional constrictions with constricted breathing.

Each time you pause to move through the first three Focus Phrases, you'll almost certainly already be caught up in one emotion or another. Or perhaps you'll feel mostly numb emotionally. If so, and if you focus on your breathing without saying the first Focus Phrase, your meditation experience will be polluted by whatever negative emotions you bring to the meditation. However, if you first state your intent to enjoy the emerging moment, then as you focus on your breathing you will naturally be free to shift to a more enjoyable experience.

Now that you've stated your intent to enjoy the present moment, go ahead and say to yourself the second Focus Phrase: "I feel the air flowing in and out of my nose." This statement will immediately turn your attention away from all thoughts of the past and future, emotions, and imaginations, and toward clear present-moment sensations in your nose. Your awareness bubble will expand enjoyably. So far so good.

But if you linger too long and fixate on the air flowing in and out of your nose, difficulties can arise. In traditional Hindu and Buddhist meditation, people are often asked to focus intently on the flow of air in the nose for the duration of the meditation. In contrast, my advice is not to fixate overmuch on the breath sensations in the nose but instead to continue expanding your awareness bubble.

Why? Because if you stay focused only on this breathing experience in the nose, you'll likely sink back into everyday thought and cease meditating. Instead, after just a breath or two, say the third Focus Phrase and encourage your awareness to continue expanding: I also feel the movements in my chest and belly as I breathe.

Notice that, when you state your intent to expand your attention another notch, your awareness bubble does expand. Say it. Do it. While staying fully aware of the breath sensations in your nose, also become acutely aware of the movements in your torso. Experience your ribs expanding and contracting with each breath, your belly moving out and in as you breathe, your skin expanding and contracting as well, your diaphragm muscle contracting and relaxing. Your pelvis may also rotate slightly to and fro as you breathe in and out.

Pause again for a few moments. Say the third Focus Phrase anew to yourself, and observe from the inside how your awareness responds to this statement of intent:

*I also feel the movements in my chest and belly as I breathe.*

## DIAPHRAGM AWAKENING

What specifically generates the constant expansion and contraction of your torso as you breathe? Thousands of muscles surrounding your ribs and spine are partly responsible for this pulsating movement. But the primary powerhouse that drives your breathing is the fairly large, flat, horizontal muscle located between the bottom of your lungs and the top of your stomach: the diaphragm muscle. In traditional chakra meditation, the region of this muscle is identified as the seat of the third chakra, located in the solar plexus.

While living in West Berlin during the early eighties, I studied with a brilliant and deeply inspiring breath therapist named Ilse Middendorf. She was elderly but still actively teaching her unique approach for using breath awareness to stimulate spiritual insight and emotional healing. I remember my experience when she first began to guide my attention to the physical presence of my diaphragm muscle as I breathed. I was lying on my back, and she was sitting with her hand on my solar plexus, telling me to just relax and experience. But the more I tried to be aware of my diaphragm muscle in action as I breathed, the more frustrated I became.

"Please, Johannes," she told me, "you cannot 'try' to be aware. You cannot force yourself to be conscious. All you can do is hold your focus in worthwhile directions, surrender — and be open to new experience."

Those words have remained with me ever since. And I say the same to you. Don't try to "make yourself aware" of your breathing. Just say over and over again, as if you're leading your horse to water, the third Focus Phrase, which returns your awareness to the movements in your chest and belly as you breathe. Each time you do this, if you are responsive and making no effort, a new experience will come to you.

*Each moment does bring*
*what you need to be aware of...*
*if you are open to receive.*

## BREATH BEFORE HEART

During my Berlin days, I was busy working as a therapist in the therapeutic tradition of Wilhelm Reich, in which emotional release is considered primary, and expressing the feelings of the heart central to emotional healing. So even as I was exploring Osho's meditative focus and Ilse's therapeutic focus on the diaphragm muscle and third chakra, I often wanted to jump from breath awareness to heart awareness because I perceived the fourth (heart) chakra as most important in my therapy practice and meditation.

This, of course, is the traditional Christian approach to contemplation, and the Buddhist approach as well. In general, people practicing meditation seem to want to focus immediately on their heart center, without first fully engaging with their breath center. The result is that they often have great difficulty connecting with their heart, because they haven't first gone through this natural awareness-expansion process that begins with the breathing.

I hope to advance a new psychological understanding of meditation by clarifying the importance of focusing first on the nose, and on the diaphragm muscle and solar plexus, when meditating. I assure you that you will soon bring your heart into this meditative equation.

For now, please trust me when I say that it's best to open

and move through the portal of breath awareness before approaching the heart portal. Our emotions are vital to all that we do, and love is the high principle of life. But without the foundation of breath, without awareness of the diaphragm muscle, which sustains our life from moment to moment, we have limited access to the "higher" heart experience.

## ALL THOUGHTS STOP HERE

I mentioned earlier that a primary aim of meditation is to temporarily quiet the flow of thoughts every day, so that a deeper, more insightful state of consciousness can emerge. Osho expressed the quiet-mind challenge this way:

> *Meditation needs patience.*
> *You must learn to be alert.*
> *True meditation is free from thought.*
>
> *Finally when there is no thinking*
> *you can come to know directly*
> *the One hidden by your thoughts.*

As I mentioned before, the ego-based stream of consciousness can prove almost impossible to silence with traditional meditative methods. Being the son of an unstoppable inventor, I've done my best to come up with new tools to help people get the meditation job done.

Way back in 1968, I remember helping Humphrey Osmond complete a research project for the National Institutes of Health that unintentionally generated several insights about the breath that remain highly relevant. While conducting seminal research at the New Jersey Neuro-Psychiatric Institute on the perceptual parameters of schizophrenia and the mystic experience, our team stumbled on a surefire psychological way to

almost immediately quiet the mind — not by using ancient
yogic maneuvers but by employing a basic law of perception.
We observed with our electroencephalographic (EEG brain-
wave) equipment that, when subjects were instructed to focus
fully on their breathing experience in the torso, the mind shifted
naturally from its usual beta (thinking) mode to alpha (quiet-
mind perception) mode. All thoughts temporarily stopped.

As often happens in scientific research, we were so busy
looking for answers to other, seemingly more important psychological questions that, in our write-ups of the data, we
mostly overlooked our secondary observation about the power
of breath awareness to quiet the thinking mind. Only much
later did I return to this research.

Related to this core discovery (that focusing on torso
breathing quiets the thinking mind), I also remembered a late-
night, deep theoretical discussion between Humphrey Osmond
and Alan Watts, who was on the NJ Neuro-Psychiatric Institute's board and visiting the research center at the time. They
were reviewing EEG findings that suggested the human brain
operates in one of two opposite modes. At any given moment,
we focus our attention on a point (stereoscopic vision) or series
of points (deductive reasoning, etc.), or we let go of that habitual fixation on a point and expand our awareness to perceive
the whole situation or scene at once.

Humphrey's theory (which has since been proven) was that
deductive thinking requires the mind to focus closely on a point
or a series of points as we progress through a logical flow of
words, images, and concepts. In contrast, intuitive inspiration
happens when the mind lets go of point fixation and perceives
the whole at once. If you reflect on how your own mind works,

you'll probably agree. Your usual thoughts come to you as part of a step-by-step, point-by-point focus on one word or phrase or image after another (the habitual stream of consciousness), whereas intuitive flashes of insight and realization come suddenly, all at once, complete and integrated.

Alan agreed with this psychological model by insisting that, in his za-zen meditative experience, his everyday thought-flows naturally became suddenly quiet when he shifted his attention to his whole breathing experience — a vast orchestration of sensory events flooding the brain all at once.

*Experiencing one's breathing as a whole*
*naturally induces the shift*
*from point fixation*
*to "seeing everything at once"*
*and, in the process, spontaneously*
*quiets the mind.*

## TWO OR MORE SENSORY EVENTS

Years later in West Berlin, I remembered this discussion and observed (while employing Ilse Middendorf's breath meditation process) that, when I focused only on the air flowing in and out of my nose, I still stayed mostly focused on a point — the area in my nose where the sensations of breathing were strongest. As a result, my thoughts tended to dominate and disturb my meditation.

But as soon as I expanded my awareness to include the movements in my chest and belly as I breathed, I found myself focusing on thousands of different movement sensations at the same time. And my thoughts instantly and effortlessly stopped.

If you meditate, or have meditated in the past, you've prob-ably had a similar experience. As you focus on your breathing in your chest and belly, for a few moments your attention tries to shift rapidly from one sensation to another in habitual point fixation. But then you finally let go of point fixation and enter an expanded consciousness, where you experience your breath-ing process in its entirety, as a whole, integrated, "eternal now" experience.

In the process I'm teaching you, even before you go deeply into your torso-breathing experience, right when you become aware of your nose-breath sensations and say the third Focus Phrase, which expands your awareness to include your torso breathing, you will become aware of many sensations at the same time in different parts of your body. You will let go of point fixation and expand your consciousness to take in your whole breath experience at once.

All your life you've been regularly shifting back and forth from point fixation to "seeing the whole at once" and thor-oughly enjoying the fruits of that shift. For instance, when you listen to Bach or the Beatles and expand your awareness to in-clude two or more harmony lines at once, you pop into that wonderful state of consciousness in which you're temporarily transported beyond your usual thinking mind, into musical bliss.

And when you gaze at a sunset, you take in the whole. When you're making love and you tune in to multiple sensa-tions at the same time, your bubble of awareness expands to in-clude your sexual partner and the sexual-bliss moment awakens. Even while just enjoying a good meal, or while out jogging, or while enjoying any other activity where you tune in to multiple present-moment sensations at once, you will shift naturally into this expanded state of consciousness that I'm teaching you to purposefully seek, via the first phase of the Uplift meditation.

Your challenge, as you add the third Focus Phrase, is to continue to be aware of the sensations in your nose even as you also focus on the sensations of breath movement in your chest and belly. With practice, this multiple-sensation focus will enable you to tap at will into the expansive bliss of whole-body awareness.

## ZEN UPLIFT

I hope that, over the next weeks, you will delve deeply into this primary cognitive-shifting dynamic that quiets all the habitual thoughts in your mind and generates an expanded sense of spiritual wholeness and well-being. It's vital to fulfillment in life, and yet also simple. You just focus your attention on the breath-sensation point inside your nose, then expand your awareness to simultaneously include the many other breath sensations always happening in your torso. By performing this mental act, you become aware of two or more things at once, and you shift from point fixation into an experience of the whole of your breathing.

From a psychological perspective, you shift your attention from the left-hemisphere cognitive region of the brain to the right-hemisphere creative-intuitive region. You move from a two-dimensional point in space and time to a three-dimensional experience of present-moment volume. This is the primal shift that generates the Zen Uplift experience.

During the first week or two of practicing this perceptual expansion of your awareness bubble, you'll need to take time to master the shifting process. Please trust me when I say that practice makes perfect. Just continue to lead yourself through this process over and over, without taking it too seriously, until at some point the mental "pop" from two-dimensional thinking to three-dimensional experiencing starts to happen easily.

When this happens, you'll have mastered one of the primary challenges of meditation — that of choosing to become a more fully conscious person. As I noted earlier, unless you pass through the breath portal, it can be difficult to advance to the "heart" dimension of meditative experience.

*Breath meditation is a way*
*of settling into yourself*
*at the innermost core of your being.*
*Once you have found*
*the center of your existence,*
*you will have found*
*the beginning of eternity.*

— OSHO

## SHIFTING CONSCIOUSNESS GEARS

As long as your thinking mind remains dominant, you don't have full access to all the other dimensions of human consciousness. Saying the first three Focus Phrases to yourself is like pressing in the clutch on a stick-shift transmission. It lets you choose to shift into a different gear, a different function of your mind.

I highly value the cognitive thinking process of the brain, but deductive reasoning and problem solving are not the only important modes of consciousness we possess. Using Focus Phrases to quiet the flow of thoughts through your mind will transform your inner experience into a most welcome state of peace and calm. And once you shift into silent, peaceful, present-moment consciousness, you're free to focus your attention toward the more intuitive, creative, and integrative functions of the mind.

Learning to shift gears, however, takes time. Many people feel pressure to make progress fast when starting to meditate. Remember, though, there's absolutely no rush to master this process. There's no absolute enlightened state to attain. Your life will unfold as an ongoing progression deeper and deeper into your infinite spiritual being, and I've found that the best way to advance spiritually is via relaxed enjoyment of every step of the process.

So give yourself plenty of time as you explore how these first three Focus Phrases elicit the universal cognitive-shifting response. This is a giant expansion of consciousness, which you're now learning to instigate at will. And the beauty of the Uplift system is that, as Ilse Middendorf said, you don't have to make any effort. Just patiently lead your horse to water again and again, knowing that you desire to drink the water of higher consciousness or you wouldn't be doing this meditation in the first place. All you need to do is relax, enjoy, and practice the process.

## THE EXPANSION POP

Once again, let me gently ask you: are you still aware of your breathing experience as you read these words? If not, no problem. Simply expand your awareness once again to include the sensations of air flowing in and out of your nose, and the movements in your chest and belly as you breathe. Each time you return to this expansion process, it will be easier and more natural, until it becomes second nature to pop back into the present moment.

When you become lost in thought, notice that your natural

inner sense of depth perception drops away. And then, as you tune in to your breathing again, your sense of depth perception suddenly pops back into existence. This occurs because your body's sensory experience functions organically within the space-time continuum of volume.

That's why, when you're dancing, swimming, making love, cooking, or doing any other activity that involves the movement of your body in space and time, you tend to shift into the zone much more easily and have a more satisfying whole-body experience. When you're out in nature, you tend to feel more vibrant, integrated, and in harmony with what's around you than when you're lost in thought, because you've naturally shifted into a heightened awareness of your sensory presence.

At every moment of your life, wherever you are and whatever you're doing, you can always choose between a three-dimensional sensory experience and two-dimensional thinking experience. And, as I hope you're discovering through experience right now, you can stay aware of your three-dimensional breath experience even while reading these words and engaging thoughtfully.

The three Focus Phrases you have learned so far are your main tools for negotiating the shift from thought to experience whenever you want, and for maintaining experiential awareness while delving into mental reflection — just as you are doing right now.

*As you inhale, you perform*
*the primal ritual that brings new life into being.*
*And every time you exhale,*
*you express the fulfillment of a life cycle.*
*When you remain focused on the present moment,*

*you experience, with each and every breath,*
*the fullness of life and death.*

As mortal creatures, we are born and we die, and in between we breathe. If we fully accept and experience this truth,
then every new breath becomes our portal into higher engagement with our creator. This is our link with the divine and, at
the same time, with our mortality — oneness and wholeness
are found in the breath experience.

Like our breaths, which come and go, we also come and go.
And to the extent that we acknowledge and embrace our own
mortality, we become free of the primary cause of emotional
suffering — our ego's fear of dying. All the deep, spiritual
teachers I've known have said this same thing: only when you
become free from the fear of dying can you fully live and enjoy
each new breath, which comes as a gift to you. Within the ongoing natural breath cycle, you will experience healing, insight,
and love. To focus regularly on your own breathing is to maintain balance at the core of your life, so that you embrace both
ends of being — the inhalation and the exhalation.

Via meditative attention, you will gently follow your breath
beyond your fears of mortality, and educate your ego to understand the deeper truth that we all do come and go. This is how
I've come to see the breath experience, and to place such high
value on it.

## ENGAGING THE LIFE FORCE

I'd like to turn you on to a special breath meditation that I do
several times every day to stay attuned to the power that sustains me. I recommend that you make this a daily experience,
because it brings you directly into harmony with the life force.

Before we do the meditation itself, let me answer two questions that arise when most people approach meditation. First, I talk a lot about the nose and about breathing consciously through the nose. Some people wonder whether there's something holy about the nasal passages, or whether they can do breath meditation through the mouth, especially when the nose is plugged up, or when the practitioner has a deviated septum or other nasal problem.

In classic yoga meditation, breathing through the mouth, especially during meditation, is frowned on. Yoga is about control, and breathing is best controlled through the nose. Emotional expression and discharge happen mostly through the mouth, and yoga is about controlling the emotions.

But you know me — for ten years I was a passionate bioenergetic emotional-release therapist. Even while fervently practicing yoga, I was also fervently working with emotional-healing techniques that focused on breathing through the mouth in order to prompt the release of pent-up feelings. And I found that there's a time and place for both. In this, I discovered a kindred spirit in Osho, who taught his followers potent emotional-release techniques based on the teachings of Wilhelm Reich, the greatest emotional-release master of them all.

From my understanding, whenever you feel you have emotional pressure inside you, breathe through the mouth and encourage the outflow of emotion. This will lead to what I understand as emotional health. Don't hold it in. Get out and run or dance or engage in some physical sport, or make love — find a way to blow off your steam. Then you'll find that, when you do sit down to meditate, it's vastly easier to be quiet and tune in to the more subtle experience that, yes, does come through nasal breathing. Also if your nose is plugged up, rest assured that you can do these breathing meditations through your mouth.

The second question I'm often asked is about sitting. How should you sit in meditation — what's the correct posture? I wrote at length about this in *Seven Masters, One Path* — and I'll sum it up succinctly here: you must find your own seating. As Krishnamurti would advise you, don't look to a master to tell you what to do — that isn't exploration; it's servitude. Discover on your own what happens when you sit in your easy chair to meditate. I personally do it often. Also experiment to discover the difference between sitting upright in a chair and having your back slumped in a more relaxed posture. And don't forget that standing is a meditative posture, as is lying down on your back.

> *Meditation has no rules.*
> *I can give you guidelines to try,*
> *but you must choose what you like best.*
> *As Lao-tzu often quietly pointed out,*
> *change is the primary element of life,*
> *so change your meditation posture as you like.*
> *Just stay conscious of the change!*

It's true that if you return to the same corner and sit in the same posture for twenty years, you'll go deeply into whatever that place and posture evoke in you. But if you sit in a different place each time you meditate, you'll have a different yet equal experience.

Optimally, I do my best to meditate all the time, whatever I'm doing and whatever posture I'm in. If I'm aware of my breathing, alert to what's happening, then posture doesn't matter, because I'm in action and flowing with the flow. However, I do love to sit in the classic cross-legged posture once a day, on a pillow with my back comfortably upright. Let's not throw the baby out with the bathwater. Much of the traditional wisdom is right on.

Moreover, don't let a guru tell you to hold still while you meditate. Stay free to move spontaneously. In the emerging movement, you will come to find your seat and become calmer, quieter, and more centered.

Here's the meditation technique I now want to teach you, if you'd like to try it. This meditation focuses on your exhaling and then remaining empty for a moment, until you get hungry for air. Then you relax and allow the diaphragm muscle to do its thing, as you effortlessly inhale new air into your lungs. Then exhale again until you're empty...hold...and let your next breath come of its own. Experience your life force right there, breathing you. Get to know it well.

*Exhale...hold...*
*make no effort to inhale.*
*Let time go by while you're empty,*
*and then surrender to the diaphragm muscle's*
*natural impulse to contract.*
*Draw in new air and life.*
*Again, exhale...hold...experience...inhale.*

## PRACTICE MAKES PERFECT

My primary intent in writing this book and developing online video training programs related to the Uplift process, is not only to discuss the process but also to make sure you move through the actual inner experience over and over, so that you learn the process by heart. In that spirit, to end this chapter let's move through the first three Focus Phrases again. You can also go online and let my voice and visuals guide you through the experience.

Get comfortable and, first of all, choose to enjoy this moment. Focus your attention on your own physical presence, here and now.

Without making an effort, go ahead and tune in to the sensation of air flowing in and out through your nose right now. And experience your awareness bubble naturally expanding another notch as you say to yourself, "I also feel the movements in my chest and belly as I breathe."

As you continue breathing, allow your awareness to become centered in the area of your solar plexus. Explore what it feels like to hold your focus of attention here.

The diaphragm region is called your solar plexus because it is the bright power-center of your life. From your first breath at birth, the contraction-relaxation reflex of the diaphragm region plays God's role of breathing life into you.

At each new moment, right here and now, your vital third chakra, the area of your solar plexus, is keeping you alive. This is your power center, where the light of life is continually being sparked in you. As your breaths come and go, make absolutely no effort to breathe. Trust your diaphragm muscle to effortlessly sustain the pleasure of life and breath in your body.

Regularly each day, refocus your attention so you again become aware of the air flowing in, and the air flowing out, and the experience that comes deep within you when you are attuned with this flow of air. Enjoy the expanding feeling of balance and harmony happening throughout your body.

Here again your first three Focus Phases to learn by heart:

*I choose to enjoy this moment.*
*I feel the air flowing in and out of my nose.*
*I also feel the movements in my chest and body as I breathe.*

CHAPTER FOUR

# REGAIN WHOLE-BODY PRESENCE

*Without opening your door*
*you can open your heart*
*to the world.*

*Without looking out your window*
*you can see the essence*
*of the way.*

— LAO-TZU

As you've discovered by now, the act of saying the first three
Focus Phrases to yourself effortlessly expands your awareness to include the full breath experience in your head and
torso. And once you reach this point in the Uplift meditation,
there's really no stopping the next expansion — into whole-
body, present-moment awareness.

From the point of view of Zen meditation, with this fourth
Focus Phrase you fulfill the core meditative process. Zen is
about simply being here now — about becoming fully aware
of your entire organism at once, consciously breathing the air
around you while alert to all your senses, with your mind quiet
and receptive.

There will be times when the first four Focus Phrases feel

complete, and adequate to fulfill your meditative intent. It is not ordained that you must move through all twelve Focus Phrases every time you pause to wake up your soul in the present moment. You'll know intuitively, when you say the fourth Focus Phrase, whether you want to move forward with the rest of the Focus Phrases or prefer to remain quietly in this remarkable Zen state of consciousness, where there's nothing to do, nowhere to go — and all things are possible.

The fourth Focus Phrase, like the first three, states your intent in as few words as possible:

*I'm aware of my whole body at once,*
*here in this present moment.*

The first three Focus Phrases expand your awareness to include all sensations related to your breathing in your nose and torso. This fourth Focus Phrase fully expands your inner experience to include absolutely everything, from the top of your head to the bottom of your feet. It moves your awareness out into your arms and hands and down through your legs into your toes.

You will probably, as you begin to explore this fourth Uplift step, at first find your awareness jumping from one part of your body to another, shifting rapidly from point to point rather than experiencing the whole at once. This is perfectly okay in the beginning. Rest assured that each time you say to yourself, "I'm aware of my whole body at once," you'll be encouraging your awareness to move from point fixation to experiencing the entire volume of your body as a whole. The two words "at once" are a key elicitor phrase — it'll guide your awareness step-by-step in the direction you desire.

## GOING FOR VOLUME

As you may have already guessed, the fourth Focus Phrase is designed to focus your attention on the total volume of your body, as opposed to individual parts and points. If I asked you, with no preparation, to be aware of your whole body at once, you might find it almost impossible. But the Uplift process is a progressive meditation that begins with focusing on your enjoyment of the present moment, and then on your enjoyment of the breathing sensations in your body. At that point you're ready to experience the whole at once. As you become adept at this meditation, you'll find that often, even as you say the first Focus Phrase, you'll shift into the "everything at once" awareness mode. And when you say to yourself, "I'm aware of my whole body at once, here in this present moment," you'll find it relatively easy to become deeply aware of the volume of your body as a whole.

Remember that we're following the natural path of consciousness expansion, not some arbitrary process. If it weren't for the fact that our thoughts pull us away from whole-body awareness, we would be in this Zen state of consciousness most of the time.

*Consciousness loves to expand!*
*Meditation simply returns us*
*to our natural state.*

I was lucky to learn in childhood the art of whole-body awareness from the natural masters of this planet, the animals who lived all around me on my parents' and grandparents' ranches. Animals tend to "be here now" most of the time. I suspect this is one of the main reasons people like to have pets. Being with animals helps us stay alive and vibrant in the present moment, as opposed to lost in fear-based plans, worries, guilt, shame, doubt, and all the other negative, thought-generated states of mind that make us feel bad rather than good.

For example, this morning when I woke up and went to feed my old cat, for the first time since I can remember, she simply wasn't there. I've always paused and spent maybe five minutes in the morning just being with my cat, and I realized that even her absence helped me tune in to and enjoy the present moment. Perhaps you've had a similar relationship with an animal. If so, you'll remember that special whole-body, present-moment state of consciousness that you shared with your animal friend.

An interesting detail in the evolution of our society's consciousness is that, only fifty to seventy-five years ago, the large majority of Americans lived on farms rather than in suburbs and cities. This means that, previously, most people lived with natural Zen masters as their everyday guides to whole-body, present-moment meditative consciousness. Perhaps one of the reasons that mind-management programs like this one are popular these days is that few of us live with the organic environmental teachers of old — farm animals.

In honor of my beloved old feline master, let me guide you through the whole-body process I've outlined in this chapter.

First, even as you're reading these words, give yourself permission to enjoy this present moment. Feel free to go ahead and purr if you want to.

And now expand your awareness to include the breath sensations in your nose as you breathe.

Continue expanding your awareness to include the breath movements in your chest and belly.

Now say to yourself: "I'm aware of my whole body at once, here in this present moment."

## CHAKRA TOGETHERNESS

People usually tend to focus overmuch on one or two of the seven remarkable energy centers located in the head and torso. One of the important aspects of the fourth Focus Phrase is that it naturally leads you into an integrated, balanced experience of all your energy centers at once.

You won't have to do anything specific to attain whole-body chakra integration. Once you become adept at this process, you'll effortlessly stimulate chakra integration when you say to yourself, "I'm aware of my whole body at once, here in this present moment."

*The natural energetic state*
*of your seven chakras*
*is that of healthy balanced integration*
*throughout your energy system.*

Your habitual thoughts tend to pull your energetic system out of balance by focusing too much on specific chakras. In case you're not familiar with your chakras, let me quickly share with you my understanding of where they are and what they're about.

The first chakra, usually called the root chakra, is located at the base of your spine. It is the "earth" energy center that

grounds you in earthly mortal reality. My experiential understanding of the location of this chakra is that it encompasses
your pelvis, legs, and feet. When you become aware of your
whole body at once, you'll naturally be aware of your legs and
your feet as part of that whole — this seems to work best.

The second chakra is located in and around your genitals,
which for women includes the womb and ovaries. Without
sexual creation, our species simply wouldn't exist at all, and
any creative act draws on the power of this deep, organic center. Some people focus too much attention here and are over-
charged sexually. Others focus almost no attention here and
lose most of their creative charge. Each time you say the fourth
Focus Phrase, your focus will include your root chakra and
sexual chakra; this can literally change your life if you are out
of balance in this creative region of your energetic body.

The third chakra, the breath center, is located in your solar
plexus and is associated with power, with your life force, your
ability to manifest in the world. Curiously, in martial arts traditions the power center is located lower in the belly. My meditative experience suggests that two distinct energy centers seem
to make up the third chakra. You'll discover for yourself in
meditation what it feels like to experience the volume of this
third chakra, and to integrate breath and power into your full
energetic system. Some people constantly overstimulate this
power chakra, while some hardly focus on it at all. Once again,
our aim is integration and balance, which is regularly regained
by experiencing all the chakras at once through the fourth
Focus Phrase.

Above the solar plexus lies the fourth energy center, the
heart. Many people, from childhood onward, experience a great
deal of emotional pain centered in this chakra and, to avoid

this pain, stop focusing on this energy center almost entirely. Others seem so caught up in their heart emotions that they are overwhelmed by this energy center. When you do the fourth Uplift meditation, you use the power of awareness to rebalance your energy system.

The fifth chakra, located in your throat, is traditionally understood as the communication chakra, where thoughts rise up into consciousness and are expressed. Whenever you communicate vocally with the outside world, you draw on a flow of energy that starts deep in your creative center, rises up through your power center and heart, and then passes through your throat and mouth and out into the world. As I sit here "talking" this book, I'm practicing what I preach and staying aware of my whole body. This feels good! When you regularly enter whole-body awareness, you optimize the power, clarity, and creative inspiration of everything you say.

We now move up to the sixth energy center, which you have already met by tuning in to the air rushing through your nose. This center is traditionally located "between the eyes." As we have seen, though, it is not a point in space but a region within your body. To become aware of this dimension, you must temporarily silence the sort of thinking associated with the fifth chakra, so that insight and intuition can flash into existence in your mind. The fifth chakra represents linear logical thinking, whereas the sixth chakra is all about nonlinear creative insight and realization. As I explain in depth in *Kundalini Awakening*, this is also where the spiritual merges with the material.

The seventh chakra isn't something I talk about much. Certainly this "crown" chakra exists and, in some remarkable way, is our direct link with the divine, as the yogic tradition has always indicated. But in my experience, the crown chakra cannot be dealt with independently of the other chakras. In the Uplift meditation process, none of the energy centers can be isolated and dealt with on their own.

> *Your chakras are energetically*
> *indivisible from each other.*
> *And so it seems wise*
> *to relate to them as a whole,*
> *not as isolated units.*

This doesn't mean there's no value in focusing your attention periodically on each of the energy centers in turn. I recommend doing just that once a day. Regularly focusing the power of your attention on your chakras will recharge them, and this will be especially useful for those you seldom focus on. In the back of this book, you can find links to websites with short videos that will guide you through an enjoyable and effective chakra-focusing process.

After you focus on your individual chakras, it's important to always say to yourself the fourth Focus Phrase, "I'm aware of my whole body at once, here in this present moment," so that you reintegrate your energy centers.

The fourth Focus Phrase has simple, clear power — you lead your attention-horse to water and simply let it drink. The conceptual mind really has no idea how to manage your chakra system, any more than it knows how to manage your immune system or your parasympathetic system. You must trust the higher wisdom of your body and spirit to use the power of expanded awareness to regain optimum balance within you.

This would be a good time to pause and reflect on what we've covered so far in this chapter. Stay aware of your breathing throughout, and see what insights rise up within you. Consider the following questions.

- Do you trust the deeper organic wisdom of your being to naturally manage the more subtle energetic aspects of who you are and how you function?
- Do you want to take time each day to reactivate this self-balancing process through focused awareness?

*Pause and Reflect*

## ULTIMATE CHAKRA INTIMACY

While seeking insight into the true nature of meditation, I studied under at least half a dozen supposedly wise men who taught me complex concepts about meditation, chakra balancing, and kundalini awakening. But the truth is, my deepest insights into my spiritual presence came to me not from any certified guru but from a remarkable young woman named Rebecca.

When I met Rebecca, I'd temporarily returned to live in my hometown of Ojai while writing my first novel. She was working as a masseuse and was also a powerful and successful spiritual healer. I was a physical and spiritual wreck at the time. Becky and I fell in love and had a passionate, yearlong encounter, during which I healed deep emotional and spiritual wounds under her guidance.

After all my therapy training and work in the emotional-release tradition of Wilhelm Reich during the previous seven years, I'd assumed I was mostly finished with my personal emotional-recovery process. But when I began to explore the deeper realms that Rebecca guided me into, merging sexual and spiritual awakening, I realized that I'd only just begun to discover sexual love and spiritual awakening.

*With Rebecca, I discovered that,*
*when two people truly merge sexually,*
*what they're ultimately doing*
*is bringing all seven of the chakras*
*into potentially explosive communion.*

As another of my teachers from around this time, Alexander Lowen, explained in his landmark book on bioenergetics, *Love and Orgasm*, most people (at least back then) seemed to be tapping only superficial levels of orgasm in their lovemaking. Spiritually, a genuine orgasm is best described as the total union that occurs when all seven of one's chakras fire off together, in full resonance with the chakras of one's sexual partner. Rebecca led me step-by-step in a progressive surrender to that full chakra-orgasm experience.

I'd received my formal training in therapy from one of Wilhelm Reich's main disciples, a man named Chuck Kelly, whose Radix Institute was located in the Ojai Valley. While I was with Becky, I finally had to part ways with Chuck because he allowed absolutely no meditative instruction in the therapy he taught. From a psychological perspective, his emotional-healing process was probably the best on the planet; it left therapy clients fully cleansed of negative emotions. But they were then stuck in a spiritual void that, in my opinion, required a meditative conclusion to the therapy process.

Pushing beyond the conceptual limits of psychology, Rebecca led me to the discovery of something beyond what I had learned — an experience of the reality of my own energetic system, which became apparent to me during our quiet meditation together and during the explosive realizations that come with full chakra orgasm. What Becky taught me can't really be put in words — our chakras aren't concepts; they are energetic realities within our bodies. My role here, then, is simply to point your attention regularly toward the inner experience of your body as an integrated energetic organism. Say it. Do it:

*I'm aware of my whole body at once,*
*here in this present moment.*

## INSTANT CHARISMA BOOST

Let's bring this chakra discussion into everyday understanding and application. Whole-body chakra meditation is often viewed as highly esoteric, but it is equally the opposite. In daily life, you physically and psychologically operate by means of the vibratory manifestation of your unique personal life force as material expression and action. And to the extent that your energetic system is balanced and amply charged, you can succeed in the world socially and in business.

As I discuss in detail in my business book *Executive Genius*, my meditation process — the part that you've learned so far — can be put to highly pragmatic use at work or in any social situation. Whenever you feel nervous, weak, confused, or caught up in a negative emotion that might undermine your ability to relate successfully, you have the power to, in just four breaths, take charge of your energetic condition, regain your inner balance and power, and successfully broadcast your inner power and intent.

We're talking about that elusive quality called charisma —

an expanded state of consciousness in which you are fully aware of your whole body at once, well balanced in your inner energetic system, and in active harmony with the people you're relating with. When you're conscious of all seven energy centers, and broadcasting a harmonious symphony of emotional, intellectual, and social expressions, you do tend to succeed in the world.

It's the same when you're relating at romantic and sexual levels. If you're habitually stuck in one or two of your energy centers, and unable to share at other energetic levels, then it's difficult to relate to others at all. What to do? Simple. The next time you go to work or enter any other social or personal engagement, experiment with moving through the first four Focus Phrases fairly quickly, before or even during any group or one-on-one encounter. Use the following routine to gain a charisma boost:

1.  Regardless of what's happening, consciously choose to enjoy yourself in the present moment. People enjoying themselves are enjoyable to be with. So hold in your mind the first Focus Phrase: "I choose to enjoy this moment."

2.  When you get lost in thought right when you need to be focused on the people you're with, pop back into the room by saying to yourself: "I feel the air flowing in and out of my nose."

3.  Social and workplace situations can make your breathing tight and shallow, reducing your oxygen intake and making you dizzy and unfocused. To relax and expand your breathing, say to yourself: "I also feel the movements in my chest and belly as I breathe."

4.  And to bring yourself fully into a positive charis-
    matic state, with all your chakras equally balanced,
    say to yourself: "I'm aware of my whole body at
    once, here in this present moment."

Before or at any time during a business meeting or social
encounter, you can say these Focus Phrases to yourself without
anyone's knowing. So take this charisma-boost process with
you to work and to social engagements, and maximize both
your enjoyment and your success.

## CONSCIOUS SPIRIT INFLOW

To end this chapter, I'd like to share with you a special application for the first four Focus Phrases, which will augment
your ability to enjoy yourself and succeed in the world. In national polls, most Americans claim they believe in a God who is
somehow active in their lives. But what does this really mean?
How can God or Allah or Universal Mind or Great Spirit or
Buddha or Krishna actually touch and influence our inner experience and decisions? How do Spirit, by whatever name you
call it, and spiritual wisdom, power, insight, and guidance enter
our personal awareness and directly influence our lives?

When I was at seminary, we enjoyed many heated discussions on this issue of Spirit influencing individual lives. For
some Christians, the Holy Spirit is a concept, not an actual
happening. For others, Spirit is the living active ingredient
of God's presence in the world. Professor Mylenberg, in particular, insisted that he had become a Christian in midlife specifically because late one night he experienced the flow of Holy
Spirit into his heart and mind. Before that, he hadn't even be-
lieved that an experiential Spirit existed, so he wasn't imagining

or pretending anything. Then, bang — he experienced something that for him was absolutely real at a subtle, sensory, tangible level of perception. His experience was the opposite of his beliefs, so he took the courageous leap and threw out his beliefs, and focused on the experience.

Ever since those seminary days, I too have done my best to steadily throw out of my mind one belief after another, in my search for genuine spiritual experience rather than grand concepts of religious theology and imagination. I've been deeply interested in the actual experiential process through which we open up — by whatever terms we choose — and receive spiritual insight and empowerment.

In short order, let me summarize what I've found to be true, and you can take it for what it's worth:

SPIRIT INSIGHT 1. Spirit seems to flow only in the present moment. Our spiritual experience doesn't happen in the past, and it doesn't happen in the future. It happens only right here, right now. This means that the more you focus your attention on the here and now, the more available you will be to receive Spirit into your life. This is probably why most meditative traditions (as opposed to theological belief systems) focus on encouraging the shift from thinking about the past and future into present-moment awareness.

The first four Focus Phrases are a powerful tool for quickly returning your attention to the present moment. Every time you say them to yourself, you move your consciousness into optimum position to receive spiritual flow into your life. You cannot make the horse drink; you cannot force Spirit to inflow. All you can do is maintain the state of consciousness that optimizes communion with the divine.

SPIRIT INSIGHT 2. Spirit seems to flow into our lives as a full-blown, three-dimensional experience, not as a two-dimensional thought. When you are lost in thought, you are not in position to receive the inflow of Spirit. Only when you quiet your chattering ego mind can you receive communication from the spiritual depths of your being. The first four Focus Phrases quiet your mind so that you are in position to receive.

SPIRIT INSIGHT 3. In my experience, Spirit doesn't flow into any particular chakra or energy center. Many traditional spiritual teachers disagree with me on this point, but when I feel touched by Spirit, when I suddenly experience oneness with God, when spiritual insight temporarily overwhelms me, it is a whole-body experience in which all seven of my energy centers are equally touched and transformed.

The first four Focus Phrases have become for me a primary lifeline to spiritual exploration, discovery, and support. There are several additional Focus Phrases that augment the inflow of Spirit. But as you'll discover for yourself, the later Focus Phrases carry no power unless you remain fully immersed in the state of consciousness elicited by the first four.

Specifically, for the other Focus Phrases to have power you must be aware of your breathing and your whole-body presence in the here and now. That's just how it is — you gotta be here for anything to happen here. So whenever you move through the entire set of Focus Phrases, continuously remain aware of your wholebody breathing experience. And whenever you lose your breath awareness, return to the beginning and start over. After all, what's the point of moving through the full process if you are not present in the here and now to experience it?

We've covered a lot in the last few pages. This is a good time to pause, put the book aside, tune in to your breathing, and see what insights come to mind.

## THE BIG FOUR

Let me again present these four essential Focus Phrases for you to learn by heart. I hope you now understand how deeply these four statements of intent can take you, when used as ongoing mantras resonating in the back of your mind.

Say these Focus Phrases silently to yourself as you exhale; feel the words being spoken subtly with the muscles of your lips and tongue but with no audible vocalization. Then, as you inhale, experience whatever happens within you in response to these elicitor words. You'll always have a new experience, so stay open to it.

*I choose to enjoy this moment.*
*I feel the air flowing in and out of my nose.*
*I also feel the movements in my chest and belly as I breathe.*
*I'm aware of my whole body at once, here in this present moment.*

CHAPTER FIVE

# EXPERIENCE YOUR HEART

*There is no greater illusion than fear*
*and no greater foolishness than*
*preparing to defend yourself.*

*Whoever can see through all fear*
*will always be safe.*

—— LAO-TZU

We now come to what many people consider the very heart
of meditation: the process of focusing your attention directly on a deep encounter with the center of love in your body
— the region of your physical heart. Ram Dass, a teacher of
mine back when he was still called Richard Alpert, expressed
the spiritual relationship of the heart and mind this way:

*When the heart is open*
*It's easier for the mind*
*To be turned toward God.*

Focusing on and opening the heart is a dramatic and challenging act of consciousness, so don't be surprised if you feel
uncertain or even apprehensive as we approach the fifth step in

the Uplift meditation. Often people have a remarkably difficult time shifting their attention to their inner feelings. Over the years, I've gained deep compassion for anyone facing the leap of faith into heart meditation — and I assure you we're going to move gently in this chapter.

I wrote a whole book, *Let Love Find You*, on this heart theme. In this chapter I've condensed that discussion and added new dimensions that will help you quickly enter into deep, positive meditative communion with your own heart. I hope you take plenty of time to fully explore this fifth Focus Phrase and the amazing portal that will open every time you say the Focus Phrase.

First, let's do a test run to discover your present relationship with the feelings in your heart. Begin as usual by relaxing and giving yourself permission to feel good right now. Tune in to the sensation of air flowing in and out of your nose. Expand your awareness to include the movements in your chest and belly as you breathe. And expand your awareness again, to include your whole body at once, here in this present moment. Now, while you remain in this whole-body consciousness, say to yourself the following Focus Phrase:

*I am ready to experience the feelings in my heart.*

## ARE YOU REALLY READY?

This Focus Phrase carries great power. As you stay aware of your breathing while reading these words, let's look closely at its three active ingredients:

1.  When you say "I am ready," you are clearly positioning yourself for action — you're preparing to make an inner leap.

2.  With the next words, "to experience," you clarify that you aren't going to simply philosophize about the Hindu heart chakra or Christian compassion — you're going to open up and directly experience something.

3.  That "something" is none other than "the feelings in my heart," an encounter with whatever emotions you happen to be nurturing or are stuck in.

As you say this Focus Phrase, one of two things will happen. Either you'll open up and experience the feelings in your heart, or you'll avoid those feelings. If you're feeling good, it'll be enjoyable to tune in to them. But if, for one reason or another, your feelings are painful or otherwise negative, you'll tend to avoid the upsetting emotion gripping your heart.

In this chapter I'll show you a surefire away to successfully approach this meditation on your heart, regardless of the emotions you bring to the meditation.

## EMOTIONAL TRANSFORMATION

First, let's get a few psychological facts straight. The feelings in the region of your heart, both good and bad, might seem to be purely emotional, but they have a definite physiological cause. Research has shown that, when your heart is "broken" and you feel a terrible aching in your chest, your heart muscles are in fact painfully tensed and experiencing reduced blood flow and oxygenation. Heartache is without question a genuine physiological ache.

Conversely, when you feel good in your heart, the muscles in and around it are relaxed and do feel good. There's no separating the emotional from the physiological, because emotion is a complex cognitive-biological phenomenon expressed and experienced throughout the body.

Please note that I will never ask you to focus on your physical heartbeat. Doing so could be counterproductive to the meditative experience. Instead, the words of the fifth Focus Phrase help you experience the ongoing deeper feelings, both emotional and physical, that you find in your heart region. Your job is to stay tuned in to your breathing and, at the same time, to expand your awareness to include whatever physical-emotional feelings you find in the general region of your heart.

I'm sure you've noticed that many people become ensnared in painful emotions that grip their hearts. One aim of this Uplift meditation is to help you acknowledge emotional pain and transform your negative feelings into positive ones. The transformation happens spontaneously. As mentioned earlier, the very act of aiming your loving attention at a particular internal region stimulates a healing and rebalancing process in that region. This is one of the basic "attention truths" of this meditation process and, indeed, the meditative tradition of the world: positive loving attention, focused directly on where we hurt, stimulates spontaneous healing.

If you chronically focus away from the pain in your heart in order to avoid that pain, you seriously undermine the possibility of recovering from it. That's one main reason many people don't readily recover from emotional trauma.

Each time you come to this fifth Focus Phrase, you have the wonderful opportunity to choose to open up and actively let go of the negative feelings in your heart. By mobilizing the healing power of your spiritual attention where it's most needed, you can progressively free and heal yourself each new day.

## PARADOX RESOLVED

My early mentor in San Francisco, Alan Watts, an adherent of the Zen tradition (and a near genius in the realm of philosophy), regularly pointed out that, very often in spiritual exploration, paradox raises its hoary head. It demands that we push beyond the logic of the deductive mind and consider an expanded spiritual logic. Ram Dass agreed, saying,

*Across planes of consciousness*
*we have to live with the paradox*
*that opposite things can be*
*simultaneously true.*

A key paradox is the psychological fact that, in order to provoke positive change, you must first fully accept a situation just as it is. If you deny an existing negative situation, such as a broken heart, you are, by definition, disengaged from the reality of that situation and won't be able to change it.

This is dramatically evident when dealing with negative emotions you find in your heart during meditation. If you deny or argue with negative emotions that cause you pain, you'll never actively transcend them.

Your first step is always to look honestly and acknowledge whatever feelings you find in your heart, positive or negative. Don't judge them, don't try to make them disappear. Do exactly what the fifth Focus Phrase suggests: be open to simply experiencing the feelings in your heart.

Here's my promise: when you tune in to and accept your present emotional and spiritual condition while focusing on your heart, the power of your focused attention will evoke the beginnings of emotional healing and spiritual awakening. The positive impact of the Uplift meditation process is largely the result of the paradoxical truth that you first must accept reality in order to change it.

Take some time off from reading now, and say this Focus Phrase again. Be sure to stay aware of your breathing both in your nose and in your torso. Say the Focus Phrase several times to yourself. See what happens when you open up right now and experience, without judgment, your current emotional condition: "I am ready to experience the feelings in my heart."

## IDENTIFY THAT FEELING

You will probably move through three phases as you approach the fifth Focus Phrase:

1. During the first week or so of training with the fifth Focus Phrase, you'll often want to spend a few minutes, rather than just a few breaths, with this step while meditating, taking time to actively identify the emotions you find in your heart.
2. Once you start to get good at this process, you'll find that, in just a few breaths, you can identify your dominant feelings.
3. After a few weeks' practice, in just one or two breaths you'll experience and acknowledge (and if you want to, let go of) your emotional condition at the moment.

In the beginning, when you say, "I am ready to experience the feelings in my heart," you'll find it helpful to put your thinking mind to work by consciously labeling the emotions dominating your heart. A simple "either-or" labeling process, which I am about to present, works best for this. Your job is to read each choice and quickly get a feel for which word best expresses how you feel in your heart at the moment.

For the next week or two, at least once a day, please advance through the first five Focus Phrases step-by-step. When you say, "I am ready to experience the feelings in my heart," move down the list of either-or choices and identify and accept your dominant feelings.

Try this right now. Remember to stay with your breathing throughout this process, so that you focus on the actual experience you're labeling, rather than simply thinking about the feeling.

In your heart, decide which of the following you feel:

Contracted... or... expansive
Anxious... or... trusting
Heavy... or... light
Bad... or... good
Frustrated... or... satisfied
Numb... or... responsive
Angry... or... loving
Depressed... or... joyful
Rejecting... or... receptive
Yearning... or... fulfilled
Isolated... or... connected
Unhappy... or... happy

## THE ETERNAL CONSTANT

At some point in your meditations, you'll probably enter into an unexpected experience of pure bliss in your heart and a euphoric mystic peace, where all the positive feelings explode deep within you. Wonderful — but be sure you don't then try to repeat that same experience.

As mentioned before, many people drop out of meditation because they have a remarkable experience while meditating, then try to repeat it (which is impossible) over and over again — without success. In doing so, they fail to tune in to the emerging present moment, and become frustrated and bored with meditation.

Let's be very clear about a particular psychological dynamic that can make you or break you in meditation, and in all of your life. Your experience in the present moment is, by definition, continually changing and evolving.

*You never have the same experience twice*
*because you're constantly entering*
*into a new moment*
*that's never happened before.*

In sharp contrast, your thinking mind has the ability to return to a memory or an idea, attitude or belief, fantasy or projection, and repeat that same cognitive process over and over without any change at all. People often become chronically fixated on habitual ego thoughts and self-generated imaginations, instead of focusing on the newness of each emerging moment. Then they become bored with their inner feelings because these feelings are being stimulated by habitual thoughts and attitudes

— and if they continue having the same thoughts and attitudes, they'll definitely remain stuck in the same old emotions.

In this light, we can see the radical difference between a theological religious life (built on established thoughts and beliefs, past religious events, and fantasies and projections about future religious experiences) and a meditative spiritual life that focuses regularly, beyond all thoughts, on the newness of the emerging moment. Said from a psychological point of view: belief is a function of the mind focused on the past and future; spiritual experience is a present-moment function of the mind.

Even though each new moment of God's creation brings unending change to the world, the intent of religion is, by definition, to establish a particular unchanging cognitive belief system — and to fight (sometimes to the death) to maintain and promote that static belief. Religion, seen from objective analysis, is based on worship of the past, and is often also a shared fantasy projection into the future.

The intent of meditation and spiritual exploration is to put aside concepts and beliefs that can be frozen in time, and to embrace pure spiritual experience — which by definition is always new and changing. It took me years to realize this, but once I did, and once I saw that I had to make a choice, there was no choice. The freedom and communion and empowerment of living in Spirit (always a present-moment experience) was what I always desired most.

I remember attempting to fit myself into my family's religious tradition as a Presbyterian, and, as I noted earlier, to become a minister in that faith. But soon after I finished my seminary studies and started working in a church, I found myself butting heads with certain Christian leaders who perceived my interest in meditation as a serious threat to their religion.

The administration of the San Francisco Theological Seminary had mostly supported my youthful passion to bring a meditative dimension into the Presbyterian community. They had given me a budget to set up a meditation room at the seminary. They had eagerly responded to my suggestion that Alan Watts teach a course at the seminary focused on Christian contemplation. And they even allowed us to have a weekly yoga class taught by the Hindu teacher Kriyananda.

My troubles with established religion began when I took a formal position as a youth minister with the San Rafael Presbyterian Church, just a few miles down the road from the seminary. There were only four high schoolers in the youth group when I took over that position. Six months later, when I was teaching my youth group yoga and meditation, there were forty-two participants.

But I was suddenly attacked theologically, publicly accused of heresy, removed from my job, denied communion, and kicked out of the church community. Yet what I taught was not in any way in conflict with what I perceived to be the teachings of Jesus. I had simply encouraged Christians to put aside their intellectual assumptions about their chosen religion, and open their hearts directly to the inflow of spiritual insight and Jesus's direct guidance.

I'm still suggesting basically the same thing, within a secular meditation structure that people of any religious belief system can readily put to use. Jesus taught love as the supreme spiritual truth. All religions claim to focus deeply on love as God's primary earthly manifestation in our hearts. But nearly all religions are dominated by theological belief systems, which are limited intellectual creations of the cognitive mind, not spontaneous inspired emanations from the heart.

If Christians, Jews, and Muslims focused less on their religious beliefs and more on spiritual communion with the divine, this world would rapidly evolve into a more loving, peaceful, and enjoyable place. Denying the heart's guidance leads to emotional and physical pain and sorrow. And the only true healing — for an individual or a nation or a religion — is to look honestly to the heart and let Spirit heal whatever attitudes and beliefs stand in the way of unleashing true love on this planet.

I've just said some fairly controversial things; they reflect my personal understanding. Take time right now to pause, put the book aside, and contemplate your own inner feelings about religion versus spirituality.

*Pause and Reflect*

## HIGH HEART VERSUS LOW HEART

Of all the spiritual teachers I've known, perhaps the deepest guide on my personal path was a young Burmese fellow named Thakin Kung. He suddenly appeared out of the blue in San Francisco in the early 1970s, alone with no money or friends or support group. Within weeks, doing nothing but quietly speaking his inspired truth, he had followers and supporters and was teaching an ever-growing group of students in a big old house donated to him.

I was one of those students, and every moment I spent in his presence was a remarkable inspiration and awakening. Then one spring morning, about three months after he appeared, he was gone. As far as I know, he was never heard from again.

Over and over while guiding us in meditation, Thakin pointed out that in his experience the true heart chakra is not located low down in the heart region where our everyday ego emotions chronically grab at us. He gently suggested that there is a "low heart" and a "high heart" in each person's chest. At any given moment, we can choose to focus our attention on the confusing ego emotions chronically provoked by our habitual fears and conflicts (low heart), or we can live higher up, in the true seat of love and spiritual inflow, in what he called the high heart.

Thakin taught that we cannot be focused on fear and love at the same time. Jesus and Buddha and many astute psychologists have all said the same thing. Fear and love are entirely different functions of the mind, as brain scans demonstrate. Note that all twelve of the negative emotions I listed on page 101 (in the either-or pairings) are in fact fear-based emotions that the ego stirs up by means of anxious thoughts. All twelve of the positive emotions that I listed are love-based feelings experienced in the high heart. To feel bad is to be caught up in fear. To feel good is to live in love.

Thakin encouraged us to regularly acknowledge and aim God's healing touch at our old fears — and then to choose to shift our attention away from the chronic turmoil of emotions in the low heart upward into the spiritual realm of love-based experience.

Please remember that the fifth Focus Phrase builds on your recent experience of saying the first four Focus Phrases to yourself. You start the meditation by saying, "I choose to enjoy this moment." By the time you come to the fifth Focus Phrase and say, "I am ready to experience the feelings in my heart," you will probably already have begun to shift your attention to the high heart — to feeling expansive, trusting, light, good, satisfied, responsive, loving, joyful, receptive, fulfilled, connected, and happy in your heart.

All these feelings, like the negative feelings, are always available in your heart — it's your choice. Your ultimate inner power lies in your ability to shift your attention to the high heart's love-based feelings whenever you want to.

Discover for yourself, through this meditative process, what is true for you as you regularly refocus your attention to your heart, quiet your mind, and open yourself to new experience.

Again — say it. Do it. Pause and tune in to your breathing, and say to yourself:

*I am ready to experience the feelings in my heart.*

## NEGOTIATING THE DOWNSWINGS

Before we go any further, let me speak honestly about the fact that these twelve Focus Phrases should never be seen as a cure-all that will work emotional miracles every time you apply them. For most people most of the time, we can confidently predict that the process of moving through this self-guided meditation will produce an uplift in emotional and spiritual consciousness. But there are times in most of our lives when we crash emotionally and spiritually and cannot expect an instant uplift by any means.

As mentioned earlier, there will probably be times when you say to yourself, "I choose to enjoy this moment," and the uplift will simply fail to occur. This happens to me at least a few times each month, when I'm caught up in extreme situations and simply must wait out the downswings before I catch my next updraft.

One of the greatest spiritual books of all time, the *I Ching*, teaches that there are sixty-four basic situations in which human beings find themselves. Life is continually changing, and we must learn to accept downswings along with the upswings. If you aren't familiar with the *I Ching*, I strongly recommend reading it to get a deeper feeling for this ancient Chinese wisdom regarding how to approach each of the sixty-four situations that life seems to throw at us, or bless us with, on a regular basis.

When you feel so low that you can find no joy or pleasure in the present moment, do not try to manipulate your way out of that low ebb of emotional and spiritual consciousness. The wise move is to fully acknowledge, accept, and experience how you feel. Ram Dass gave this advice:

> *The next message you need*
> *is always right where you are.*
> *Everything in your life is there*
> *as a vehicle for your transformation.*

If working with the Focus Phrases helps you move beyond an emotionally debilitating experience, great. If not, you have two choices. The first is to just wait it out: this too shall pass. Just "be" with your feelings; honor the fact that life does include these low emotions. Stay tuned in to your breathing, and see if the natural healing process moves you, step-by-step, out of your anxious or depressed feelings. The next three Focus Phrases that I introduce are designed to help you quickly let go of negative feelings and move into a brighter inner space.

If you are seriously stuck in anxious or depressed feelings, I strongly advise you to also seek out the help of a friend who will listen without judgment. Reach out to others. And of course, if the condition persists, the wise move may be to seek out professional help.

## HEALING MEDITATION

I've talked quite a bit in this chapter about the universal human dilemma of getting stuck in painful heart spaces, where you feel depressed, angry, guilty, frightened, or other negative emotions. Now let's focus on the opposite. A primary goal of all meditation is, after all, to lighten and heal the heart.

*People meditate because it makes them*
*feel better in their hearts.*
*The more you meditate,*
*the better your own heart will feel.*

We never eliminate negative traumatic memories. We all have a host of negative memories that can grab our attention and drag us down. But we can also take charge of our minds and shift our attention regularly in more positive directions. Emotional healing means fully accepting all our past experiences, forgiving others and ourselves, devoting loving attention when an old emotional ache needs to heal — and not fixating on past memories and emotional upsets.

The twelve Focus Phrases are structured to help you actively choose to shift your attention and nurture the flow of healing love and Spirit into your heart. The fifth Focus Phrase initiates healing by enabling your full, loving acknowledgment of your current feelings. The sixth Focus Phrase helps you let go of worries and anxieties so that you nurture inner peace. The seventh Focus Phrase helps you progressively let go of negative attitudes about relationships, so that you can interact with love. And the eighth Focus Phrase helps you progressively love yourself unconditionally.

These Focus Phrases will serve you very well as a long-term, daily self-therapy program. They cover all four of the primary areas of therapy, aiming your attention directly at resolving and transcending the universal, fear-based, neurotic mental patterns that plague us all. Moving quickly through these second four phrases will promote emotional wellness and prepare you for the ninth and tenth Focus Phrases, which enable you to experience deep meditation and spiritual awakening — which in turn nurture inner healing.

The ultimate aim of this Uplift process is to enable you to enjoy a loving, receptive, meditative state of consciousness throughout each day. Your heart region lies at the center of this experience, as Spirit flows into, and radiates outward from, your personal being. So take time each day to strengthen your meditation muscle. Use these mind tools to develop powerful new habits that will set you free.

To end this chapter, repeat again the phrases you've learned so far in the Uplift meditation:

*I choose to enjoy this moment.*
*I feel the air flowing in and out of my nose.*
*I also feel the movements in my chest and belly as I breathe.*
*I'm aware of my whole body at once, here in this present moment.*
*I am ready to experience the feelings in my heart.*

# CHAPTER SIX

# MOVE BEYOND ANXIETY

*If you do not accept reality*
*then you reject it.*
*And if you reject reality*
*what is left?*

*This is the choice —*
*to live in a world of illusion and self-delusion*
*or to move into the world of awareness*
*through continuing acceptance.*

— CHARLES MACINERNEY

In earlier books, I've written extensively about the best therapeutic processes for overcoming anxiety; in this book I offer a more positive, spiritual approach to "just saying no" to stress and anxiety. With the right cognitive tools and meditation habits, it's not usually necessary to approach habitual worries via formal therapeutic techniques.

If you move through this full Focus Phrase process at least once each day, you'll strengthen your ability to shift your attention away from stressful, anxious thoughts to a more peaceful, uplifted state of consciousness.

Krishnamurti spoke often about the necessity to let go of fear in order to evolve spiritually; he also clarified the core benefits of living without anxiety:

*A person who is not afraid is not aggressive.*
*A person who has no sense of fear*
*of any kind*
*is a free peaceful person.*

With the sixth Focus Phrase, there's no room for hemming and hawing about how to deal with anxiety and stress. All you're required to do is simply state your intent to shift out of fear mode altogether — and then do it. So let's get right to this new Focus Phrase. Go ahead and say it to yourself a few times and gain a taste for the power of these words:

*I let go of all my stress and worries*
*and feel peaceful inside.*

## SEEING THROUGH FEAR

Whether you like it or not, you came into this world hardwired with a reflexive neurological system that instantly goes on red alert when you perceive danger. Your system leaps into action to overcome that danger.

The amygdala region in the brain, also called the primitive fear center, dates back to an earlier period in our evolution, having first evolved in our reptilian ancestors. This ancient, fear-based, knee-jerk part of the human brain still serves a certain limited purpose in contemporary life, but it also continually causes us trouble. Why? Because the amygdala cannot tell the difference between a real danger facing you in the present moment and an imagined situation in your mind.

Imagination, the same mental function that enables human

beings to be so creative and productive, often generates fearful fantasy scenarios about the future that keep you gripped by unnecessary stress and anxiety. But my observation (and that of most therapists) is that, most of the time, you have the cognitive ability to quiet those anxious thoughts and move into a more peaceful, enjoyable, productive state of consciousness.

This is what meditation is about — change your focus, change your life. Our fifth Focus Phrase is entirely in harmony with this approach.

> *Do you have the power to say to yourself,*
> *"I let go of all my stress and worries"*
> *and in fact instantly let go?*
> *Can you just say no to fear?*

My experience is that, with a little bit of training, most people most of the time do have the power to just say no to their worries. Ultimately it's a matter of choice — and action. But please note that I'm not suggesting you try to turn off your primitive fear center altogether. There are times every day when it's vital to respond to the wake-up signal of fear. And a certain amount of time spent imagining potentially dangerous situations can keep you from getting hurt. But almost always, habitual worrying about the future is dangerous to your health, for four reasons:

1.  Every moment spent focusing your power of attention on an imagined future event is a moment when you're not here in the present to deal with dangers that might appear right now.
2.  When you're caught up in worry, your body reacts with a host of fear-based neurological and

hormonal secretions that, if not released in immediate physical action, generate stress conditions
that make you weak and dizzy, cloud your brain,
and leave you unable to successfully deal with danger in the present moment.

3. When you're stuck in worry mode, your overall
performance at work drops, your ability to relate
successfully is reduced, and your capacity to feel
compassion is lost. Both your company and your
family suffer as a result — and so do you.

4. At deeper levels, anxiety prevents you from receiving insight, love, power, and guidance from your
spiritual core. Your consciousness contracts, and
you're all alone — which in turn makes you feel
anxious and depressed.

To see these facts clearly is to evoke positive change in
yourself. One of my most deeply beloved yoga teachers and
spiritual guides, an American fellow named Joel Kramer, was
the first person to point out to me that the very act of seeing
something clearly stimulates an inner response where needed.
Perceiving a tree falling toward your head prompts you to
jump away from that danger. Likewise, the very act of seeing
your worry habits as dangerous to you will stimulate the act of
letting go of the worries.

For all these reasons, I'm here to encourage you to make
the sixth Focus Phrase your antiworry mantra for the rest of
your life. Once more: Say it. Do it. "I let go of all my stress and
worries, and feel peaceful inside."

## WHERE TO FOCUS

First, let's return to your ongoing intent to stay aware of your breathing while you read this book — how are you doing? Have you noticed that your breathing changes in depth, pace, and so forth in response to emotions that my words and thoughts provoke inside you as you read?

As you continue to feel the air flowing in and out of your nose, and the movements in your chest and belly as you breathe, let's explore how this new Focus Phrase can free you from habitual anxiety and tension. In my experience, just saying to yourself the first half of the phrase, "I let go of all my stress and worries," doesn't get the job done. Saying no to the negative isn't sufficient to generate a positive shift. You need to give your mind a new place to focus, an alternative, positive realm of consciousness to highlight: "...and feel peaceful inside."

Like *love* and all other extremely powerful words, *peace* may seem to have become a cliché, and its power lost forever — but I don't accept this. Just because advertising media and religious movements have turned a powerful word into a banal cliché doesn't mean we can't take this word back.

I suggest we return the word *peace* to its proper spiritual and psychological pinnacle, because we need a clear, strong term that expresses the universal inner feeling. What's the point of meditation if not to nurture inner peace in our hearts and souls? And we can't really experience love unless we have some peace in our hearts. That's why this Focus Phrase precedes the next two, which focus on acceptance and love.

Notice that the words "I let go of all my stress and worries, and feel peaceful inside" do not focus on the philosophical and social qualities of peace. We're talking about the actual bodily and spiritual feeling itself, not intellectual ruminations about peace as a lofty idea. In the previous Focus Phrase, I encouraged you to simply tune in to the feelings inside you. With this new Focus Phrase, I encourage you to make a clear shift in the positive direction of experiencing inner peace.

You are again leading your horse to water — you're pointing your attention in a desired direction. I've yet to find anyone who doesn't want greater inner peace. But we live in a seriously stressful world society where, even when we have time to just be at peace, we tend to focus on the opposite of inner peace. It's no secret that we're junkies when it comes to chronic sensory stimulation. Every moment of relaxation time tends to get gobbled up by television, the computer, and other diversions.

I suggest you avoid chronic perceptual stimulation. Drama on TV makes your breathing tense. Watching the news like-wise generates the opposite of calm, good feelings inside you. Worrying about the future destroys inner peace. So does dwelling on old memories that make you feel angry, guilty, or depressed.

*"I choose to feel peaceful inside."*

How often do you make this choice?
Where do you feel peace inside you?
Does the flow of Spirit into you bring peace?
Why choose to feel peaceful?
What does peaceful breathing feel like?
Can you shift into peaceful breathing right now?

## DEADLINE OR LIFELINE?

Deadlines seem to generate most of our stress. The pressure of time is killing us, and we run around "like chickens with their heads cut off," as my granddad would have put it.

*We live in a hi-tech society*
*with thousands of timesaving devices*
*designed to open up free time —*
*but does anyone have free time?*

During one phase of my psychological work, I conducted studies as a research hypnotist. Most people think hypnosis operates only by slowing individuals down and putting them in a trance, where they become highly suggestible. But as Hitler demonstrated so magnificently, hyperhypnosis works just as well as the slow-motion version. When people are speeded up, anxious, and chronically overstimulated, they lose their ability to think clearly for themselves, and become easy to manipulate. In our manic society, we seem to have acquired this condition of hyperhypnosis.

The sad thing is that we seem willing to participate in this semiconscious rat race even though it means sacrificing our spiritual wellness and pure enjoyment of life in the process.

However, I'm confident that once we begin to wake up and see this clearly and realize the danger we are in, we'll purposefully refuse chronic stimulation and instead seek inner peace and spiritual groundedness. (One reason I've written this book and produced a parallel set of meditation training programs is to make the necessary tools openly and inexpensively available for all who want to apply them to their lives.)

In my work with corporations (which I outline in *Take Charge of Your Mind* and other books), I found that most working people have the power to gain relief, wellness, more fun, and higher profits by easing up and slowing down just 10 to 15 percent. Even that small reduction in pace can make the difference between hurrying blindly and stressfully forward and moving more consciously and enjoyably through the workday.

I encourage you to experiment with this by applying the following process whenever you're on the job:

1.  Notice how often you rush manically forward, focused maybe only five to ten seconds into the future, rather than existing fully here in the present moment.

2.  When you find yourself in a rush, remember to simply *tune in to your breathing* and whole-body experience, and then silently say to yourself, "I let go of all my stress and worries, and feel peaceful inside."

3.  As you continue with your work, be sure to stay aware of your breathing experience — and hold the words "I feel peaceful inside" in your mind. Go ahead and spread peace throughout your workplace.

As you remember to ease up enough to become aware of your own physical and emotional presence, you'll find that you can still work fast and even do better work — and break free from the stress and deadline pressures that destroy the quality of inner peace in your heart and soul.

Wherever you are, just remember to regularly hold in your

mind your inner dictum: "I let go of all my stress and worries, and feel peaceful inside."

*Always, your choice...stress or peace.*
*Always the power to shift toward the light.*
*Always the freedom to choose to feel good.*
*Peace feels good!*

## ALL TOGETHER NOW

I've recently worked on an exciting application for the Focus Phrases for employees in the hospital environment. It's a tragedy that nurses and other hospital employees work under such pressure-filled conditions that they commit errors and cause suffering and even death among the very patients they're dedicated to serving.

To help alleviate this situation, several of my Focus Phrases are now being used nationwide in the context of employee mindfulness training, which is exactly what hospital employees need in order to do their work without making errors. Mindfulness simply entails paying attention. And what needs more attention is what's happening in the present moment.

In essence, all that this new employee-mindfulness program does is encourage employees to slow down just enough so that they don't get ahead of themselves and lose vital awareness of what is happening in the here and now. This is accomplished, as you may have already guessed, by teaching them to be aware of the air flowing in and out of their noses and the movements in their chests and bellies as they breathe, and by encouraging in them a heightened awareness of their whole-body presence as they go about their duties in the hospital.

In your own work life, whenever employer or peer pressure makes you speed up so much that you lose contact with your own inner spiritual presence, you're actually denying yourself access to your soul. As Krishnamurti used to point out, no one has the right to deny you your sense of an inner spiritual presence — and when they do, it's time for revolution.

I find it curiously comical that we must have a revolution in order to regain our own senses. But when we are overly hurried and chronically pushed beyond our natural conscious limits, that's exactly what happens — we lose our sensory contact and responsiveness to the present moment and our own center. We do have the right to revolutionize the workplace when it takes away our right to enjoy our present-moment experience.

The revolution I'm talking about is a quiet, peaceful one, an inner process that is entirely benign — but one that will powerfully change the world for the better, one person at a time. This will be a rapid, purposeful evolution of the human mind, which entails using it in a more conscious way to achieve a more peaceful, loving, creative performance level. Activating our capacity to provoke this conscious evolution in ourselves seems to be our primary communal hope at this point.

To that end, the next time you go to work or participate in a social group or relate with family and friends, do your best to remain conscious and at peace inside your own heart and soul even while you actively participate in your work or social situation.

Each time the pace or tension of a situation violates your spiritual peace and centeredness, choose to focus inward and say to yourself: "I let go of all my stress and worries, and feel peaceful inside."

## A GOOD DAY TO DIE

Probably you've seen old movies about the American West where a brave Indian warrior puts aside his fear of death and chooses to fight the good fight, saying the famous words "This is a good day to die!" In truth, for any of us, this could indeed be our day to die. The mortal duration of each life is entirely uncertain. But even though any day could be our last on planet Earth, most of us are in serious denial about that fact — and we suffer with chronic anxiety as a result.

I started the previous chapter with a powerful quote from an ancient book by Lao-tzu, the *Tao Te Ching*: "Whoever can see through all fear will a ways be safe." I could likewise quote Franklin Delano Roosevelt saying, "We have nothing to fear but fear itself."

Almost always we suffer emotionally not because of a future reality that's definitely going to do us in, but because we're chronically pushing our fear button by negatively imagining the future. Our ancient reptilian brain is programmed to react in certain situations like that of a rattlesnake when threatened — that's what anger and aggression are all about. When faced with a seemingly mortal threat, we tend to let our panicky amygdala dictate our response — we either attack, run away, or lose consciousness.

But we don't have to let antiquated fear reactions run our lives. We can instead see through the fear, and free ourselves to behave consciously as spiritual beings who do not let their fear of dying turn them into anxious or violent creatures. We're surely going to die — it's just a matter of time. So why let our fear of our eventual demise ruin our lives in the present moment? While we're still alive, shouldn't we instead focus on seeing how much love and creative expression we can bring into the world?

*Always there is danger in the world,*
*and always there is love.*
*Which of these will you choose to focus on*
*at any given moment —*
*that's your serious, nonstop question*
*and continual core choice.*

I'm sure you've noticed that you often react to situations as if they were matters of life or death, even when you know on reflection that they aren't. This probably happens when you have a financial upset or are plunged into a relationship problem. It may also happen when you get sick. "Oh my god, am I going to die?" you may wonder. When you seriously overreact, you experience confusion and emotional suffering that in turn interfere with your ability to thrive.

*Only when you regularly choose*
*to manage your own mind*
*and maintain a relatively expanded awareness*
*do you have the power and freedom*
*to transcend your reptilian reactions*
*and live more fully in trust,*
*love, acceptance, and peace.*

## BEYOND EGO IMMORTALITY

It's true that your mind's ego, by definition, chronically fears death, because biologically your earthly personality will probably cease to exist when your body and brain die their mortal death and cease to function. Quite possibly, your personal identity is grounded in a much deeper, eternal quality of consciousness that transcends mortal death, a point we're exploring in this book through meditation. But still, your biological ego identity, which is based on memories stored in the brain and ideas created by your brain, will naturally freak out when something reminds it of its inevitable physical demise. Here's the good news — your ego can mature, expand its scope, gain a spiritual perspective, and begin to say no when your amygdala starts to panic.

During my first twenty years or so, when I was a practicing Christian, I held on very tightly, and often anxiously, to the belief that I would never have to die, because Jesus had died for me and forever transcended physical and personal death. More than two billion human beings on this planet fervently hold on to this belief about Jesus. In the name of honest inquiry I can't talk about fear without talking about religious fears, especially the great doubt and anxiety that Christians inherently feel because they don't know for sure whether they'll go to heaven or hell, or even if such places exist.

If Christian faith were not established, managed, and supported by the mortal ego, all would be fine. But for the ego, even if life otherwise is good and safe and peaceful and fun, there is that pervading doubt about what's going to happen to the ego personality at death. And so believers must deal with a subliminal, free-floating anxiety that subtly pollutes their waking moments with doubt and denial.

*Because it does not accept*
*its probable mortal death,*
*the ego of a believer is caught*
*each new moment*
*in the utter uncertainty*
*of the future.*

Step-by-step, I let go of the need for this belief, and for this reason call myself a post-Christian. I no longer perceive myself as a sinner, as evil by nature, and so the need for salvation no longer makes sense to me. However, I still accept a lot of Jesus's teachings, because I've had direct experience of their truth.

Through meditation I discovered that I'm perfectly okay just as I am. It's a great relief to continue my communion with Jesus, and with God as the infinite all-loving Creator of our material world, but to no longer expect to live forever as an ego personality. Who knows what'll happen at the deeper spiritual levels — I'm wide open to finding out after I die. But in the meantime, I've willingly let go of the assumption that my personal ego identity, which is based on the biochemical memories stored in my brain, will transcend physical death.

I often speak about nurturing the spiritual education of the ego. This education is important because the ego function of the mind does determine what we focus on at each new moment, and if it's focused on doubts and worries, it can't focus on compassion and the inflow of Spirit. The ego needs gentle education and direct experience of spiritual truths, so that it can realize the value of focusing regularly on the infinite reality of the eternal present moment, rather than fixating on the uncertain belief of a possible perfect heaven somewhere off in the ethereal theological future.

Again, this is just my experience, as I came to let go of most of the fears programmed into me by my religious tradition. Please consider your own experience to be as true and valuable as mine. If you hold dearly to religious beliefs that promise you eternal salvation in the future, I'm not asking you to let go of those beliefs. Each of us must choose which beliefs to hold on to and which to purposefully discard, based on whether they serve us or not. But it's important to realize that we can indeed put aside religious beliefs that do not serve us spiritually. That's true freedom.

A hallmark of Jesus's teaching, as well as Buddha's and Muhammad's and Lao-tzu's, is his assertion that inner peace is absolutely essential to the spiritual life. And inner peace comes to those who have found deep meditative truth.

*Peace is something*
*you find within,*
*and it comes only*
*when you let go of fear.*
*So let's do it!*

To end this chapter, you might find it valuable to put this book aside right now, tune in to your breathing and the feelings in your heart, and see what insights come to you in the next moments regarding life and death, and the meditative experience of total acceptance and inner peace:

*"I let go of all my stress and worries and feel peaceful inside."*

CHAPTER SEVEN

# ACCEPT EVERYONE

*The highest form of human intelligence*
*is to observe yourself without judgment.*
*To transform the world, begin with yourself.*

*If you understand what you are*
*without trying to change yourself,*
*then what you are undergoes transformation.*

*The moment you have in your heart*
*this extraordinary thing called love*
*you will discover that for you*
*the whole world is transformed.*

— KRISHNAMURTI

ocus Phrase meditation gives you at each new moment the
power to positively advance the evolution of human consciousness by managing your own mind so that you're more
receptive to inspiration and guidance from your higher source.
By consciously re-aiming and expanding your focus of attention, you can become a more intelligent, compassionate, and
creative human presence on earth. Nowhere is this opportunity
more evident than in your choice at each new moment to either
focus on judging the world around you, or on accepting, embracing, and participating in God's always-emerging creation.

Most people agree that our entire universe was at some
point created out of nothingness by an infinite intelligent

power. Absolutely everything in this universe is God's creation, and yet most of us spend a great deal of time judging parts of God's creation as bad, wrong, ugly, negative, sinful, evil, and so on.

Every time we negatively judge a person or situation, we are in essence telling God, "Hey, you really messed up on this one. This particular part of your creation sucks!"

What a thing to say to our Creator. What amazing gall our egos have, to stand in judgment of God's creation. From my perspective, to condemn anything in this universe seems to be, at the very least, highly presumptuous.

Furthermore, we cause ongoing damage because of our ingrained habit of judging rather than accepting and loving ourselves and others. In this chapter, I also want to delve into what it means, spiritually and psychologically, to quiet the judgment function of the mind as often as possible, and shift into a loving mode. As Krishnamurti put it:

> *Is it possible to love another*
> *without wanting a single thing*
> *either emotionally, physically, in any way?*
> *Love cannot exist with judgment or attachment.*
> *But when there is love in your heart,*
> *whatever you do then has beauty,*
> *has grace, is a right action.*
> *The flowering of love*
> *is meditation.*

## ANOTHER EITHER-OR CHOICE

Years ago I walked away from psychological research, which had been my primary passion in life, but I do regularly look to see what my former colleagues are discovering, especially related to how different parts of the brain interact to generate what we call consciousness. Although consciousness research is still in its infancy, a major insight has already been garnered from brain-scan research. We now know that entirely different parts of the brain light up when we're in judgment analysis mode, as opposed to when we're operating in acceptance-love mode.

At any given moment, we're either caught up in the associative process of judging ourselves and the world according to one of a host of acceptance-rejection scales, or we're activating a very different part of the brain as we accept ourselves and the world just as we are, and tap into nonjudgmental emotions such as empathy and cooperation.

It seems that psychologically we can't operate in both modes at the same time. We continually choose one mode or the other: love or judgment. And this ongoing choice has a massive impact on our personal lives and the world around us.

*Every moment we spend in judgment*
*is a moment in which we are disconnected*
*from compassion and cooperation.*

Please understand that I'm in no way discrediting the mind's judgment mode. Judgment has its time and place. The problem is that so many of us are habitually stuck in judgment mode, and we have difficulty shifting from this fear-based function of the mind into uplifting, creative, heart-based states of consciousness.

All the positive inner qualities that we seek to highlight in meditation require a temporary quieting of the judgmental thoughts that tend to dominate our minds. According to my understanding of both psychological and spiritual dynamics, only when the mental process of judgment is consciously put aside are we able to open up and receive the inflow of spiritual insight, healing, love, and joy.

The following Focus Phrase will actively aid you in making the shift from judgment to acceptance, and this will happen almost instantly once you become adept at it:

*I accept everyone I know, just as they are.*

Depending on your current situation, you can use one of two variations on this Focus Phrase instead:

*I accept the world just as it is right now,*
or
*I accept this moment just as it is.*

Judgment is a defensive mental habit that the ego holds onto and considers essential for survival. Regularly letting go of chronic judgment and replacing it with trust and love is an ongoing spiritual choice.

## WHEN JUDGMENT IS GOOD

In my own life, even after years of working with this "from judgment to acceptance" Focus Phrase daily, I still catch myself getting locked into judgmental thoughts about a person, a belief, or a situation. Unless we resort to frontal lobotomy, all of us live each moment with the high probability of getting our danger-buttons pushed.

We seldom go into judgment mode unless we feel in some way endangered by a person, idea, or situation, although the threat may be subtle. First we simply perceive something; then, if our present-moment perception is linked with fearsome past experiences, we judge negatively, react, and try to protect ourselves.

In many situations, this judgment process is clearly appropriate behavior. A more neutral term for judgment is *discrimination*: we identify the difference between one thing and another, or one person and another, and act accordingly. When we're driving and see that a traffic signal is red rather than green, we discriminate between these two colors, match the color with its symbolic meaning, and stop.

Likewise, when we judge a person negatively, we alert ourselves to the possibility that, based on an association we've made between this person and someone from our past, this person could in some way hurt or threaten us. When we say to ourselves, "I don't like this person," our ego is making the decision to steer clear of this person to avoid the risk of a problem or damage, such as emotional pain.

This might be a wise move. It's important to learn from experience so that we don't repeat errors that caused problems in the past. We also constantly decide what to expose ourselves to in the media, for instance, and that's a judgment call. Even the choice of shifting from judgment to acceptance is the result of judgment.

The trick is knowing when to actively judge, and when to stop judging and experience spontaneous engagement, fun, and love. Judgment when needed is good. Being stuck judging all the time is hell, because it prevents you from directly engaging with the world.

## THE DAMAGE DONE

When you shift from perceiving someone in the present moment to judging that person, you activate the past-future, associative, thinking function of your mind. Psychologically, in the process of evaluating and judging an experience, you temporarily disengage from present-moment participation. This means that if you continually judge everything happening around you, you remain stuck thinking about, rather than actively participating in, the potential experiences available to you.

When you're stuck thinking most of the time, you lose out on the fun and mystery and passion of present-moment engagement with the world. Curiously, this is true of both positive and negative judgment. For example, when you walk down a country lane and come upon a beautiful rose, you enjoy a wonderful sensory experience of the visual and olfactory presence of that rose. But as soon as you think the thought "What a beautiful rose," you slip into thinking about the rose and lose your direct sensory contact with it. This is true of making love too. If you are judging your performance, your heart isn't in the experience — and that's no fun.

The same situation happens when you meet someone. You either stay in relatively spontaneous present-moment engagement with that person or begin thinking about and judging the person — and in the process lose the immediacy of the unique whole-body encounter. (Something similar can happen when you enter meditation. As long as you're thinking about your inner experience and judging it, you're short-circuiting your potential for a direct experience of the divine.)

Begin to obseve that when you're busy judging someone, your heart is not open to that person, because you're engaged in a nonlove, analytical mental function. During that moment of judgment, a definite human (and spiritual) tragedy occurs. In the great equation of love in the universe, you have just reduced the amount of love by being stuck in judgment mode.

To see this clearly is to move away from judgment toward acceptance. In my understanding, this reflects what Jesus strongly expressed with his dictum "Judge not." Observe yourself judging and you'll naturally stop judging.

I recommend that you use one of the three versions of the seventh Focus Phrase many times each day. Hold this "acceptance mantra" in your mind as a constant reminder that you continually have a choice between judging the world, and fully engaging your whole heart and soul in each new experience.

Pause for a few moments if you want, tune in to your breathing and your heart, and then say these liberating statements to yourself:

*I accept everyone I know, just as they are.*
*I accept the world just as it is right now.*
*I accept this moment just as it is.*

## EQUAL BEINGS, YOU AND I

The United States Declaration of Independence, as I'm sure you know, is based on the assumption that no matter how different we might be from one another, we are all created equal. However, each of us has a unique perspective on the world, and our ego tends to assume that our perspective is the right one, and that anyone with a different perspective is wrong and inferior.

This is a natural reactive function of the ego mind, but we don't have to be dominated by this function. We can use the power of expanded consciousness to overcome our habitual and often inherited judgments of others, so that we interact at higher, more enjoyable, more compassionate and insightful levels of awareness.

Specifically, what I'm encouraging you to do is to relate to all human beings as if they are your equals. Even though others perceive the world differently than we do, we can respect their point of view as much as we respect our own. And we can do this unilaterally.

> *True community is about*
> *mutual respect for community members'*
> *differing perspectives*
> *of the same reality.*

Unless we respect others, we remain driven by fear and judgment. And while we are driven by fear and judgment, we minimize love and cooperation in our world community. Throughout history, human societies developed caste systems — rigid, judgmental hierarchies of groups of people. In response to their own cultures' hierarchies, people went around looking down on some people and looking up to others. But we can consciously decide to manage our own minds and focus more on love and less on judgment.

I remember one of my main encounters with this fellow Osho, in West Berlin back in the 1980s. I had recovered my clear eyesight after years of myopia and was teaching people how to move through a similar recovery process. I'd been invited to teach at Osho's thriving spiritual center of more than five thousand devotees in West Berlin. But I was being criticized by the center's leaders for teaching that, in order to see clearly, one must not look up to anyone, or down, but look everyone straight in the eye as an equal.

Everyone in Osho's ashram was supposed to look up to him, the great master. I was violating a core principle of the ashram by insisting that people should look Osho directly in the eye as an equal. One day Osho flew into town from India, and in my first encounter with him he wanted to know if I was the daring heretic telling his followers not to look up to him as their great spiritual master. I could only smile, look him right in the eye, and say, yep, that's how I see things.

What did he do? He burst out laughing and told me to come see him later that night. I did so and was deeply impressed by what he told me when we were alone. He explained that there were many thousands of young people, especially in Germany, who had no positive father figure to look up to. He saw his role as that of a participant in a certain phase in these young people's lives, helping them to move through the youthful process of looking up to an idealized father figure whom they could love, and who loved them unconditionally, as a good father should. Then at some point, he said, it would be time for them to discover their power to look him in the eye and realize that they too are one with the divine.

When we look up to others as if they're greater, holier, or more beautiful or enlightened than we are, we deny our own divinity. And when we look down on people, we damage their psyches. Only when we treat others as equals, and accept them just as they are, do we enable the power of love to dominate our lives and transform our world. "I accept everyone I know, just as they are."

## THE PEAR DICTUM

I've often written about the Princeton Engineering Anomalies Research (PEAR) study documenting the power of intent, and of necessity I'm going to do so again here. If you're familiar with this research, just jump past this short section; otherwise, read on. It's important to know about this serious, conclusive scientific research proving that the human brain does broadcast thoughts, symbols, emotions through a still-mysterious power that influences the performance of sensitive electronic equipment. (Google "PEAR Princeton" and read the scientific details and analysis of this ten-year study.)

In the 1980s, professor Robert G. Jahn and his team at Princeton's engineering department set out to prove that Einstein was wrong when he made his famous statement that "the intent of the experimenter influences the outcome of the experiment." To their surprise and consternation, they discovered Einstein was right. Through many thousands of experimental trials, subjects were able to focus their power of intent and influence the performance of a random-numbers generator so that it regularly generated more ones than zeros.

In double-blind ESP experiments, it was also proven statistically that, when one person mentally broadcasts a particular symbol or number while focusing on another person some distance away, the latter will make selections influenced by the broadcast. The distance between the person doing the broadcasting and the receiver did not matter: when the distance was increased, even to thousands of miles, the effect was the same. The study documented the same remarkable results with the random-numbers generator, indicating that the power of consciousness somehow operates, as Einstein predicted, outside the space-time continuum. The implications of this research for our discussion are immense.

*The PEAR research project*
*proved that, when you think*
*a negative thought about someone,*
*you broadcast that thought and hit that person*
*with your negative thought,*
*knocking him or her down*
*at a subtle inner level.*

Please don't take my word for this — go to the PEAR website and read about this research and related experiments, so that you fully comprehend the fact that thinking negative judgmental thoughts is a harmful act.

The research offers one way to understand what Jesus and Buddha were talking about when they insisted that the proper spiritual act is to accept and love rather than judge others. The Buddhist notion of living a harmless life is grounded in the deep realization that not only our physical actions but also our mental actions influence the world for better or for worse.

What do you think of this? Do you have the mental power to broadcast your thoughts and feelings into the world and subtly influence people's thoughts and feelings? Pause for a few moments if you want to, and tune in to your breathing. See what insights rise up from the center of your being.

## ACCEPTANCE AND CHANGE

Curiously, when I've presented the three versions of the "acceptance" Focus Phrases to people in workshops and seminars, about three-fourths of the participants initially reject them vociferously. So don't feel alone if a voice in the back of your brain is saying, "John really has it wrong here. I'm not going to accept the world as it is — that's crazy! I want to change the world, stop all the violence, reduce plague and famine, help the suffering poor, and boost love and prosperity for all. But now here comes John telling me I should give up trying to change the world for the better, and simply accept the terrible mess it's in right now. This is a dangerous, defeatist attitude that would let the evil forces in the world win. No way!"

I fully understand this line of logic. But psychologically it's simply not correct. As I've pointed out, our chronic judgmental-rejecting-hostile thoughts aren't helping the world. In fact, they're busy knocking it down. The last thing the world needs right now, according to my understanding, is more negative judgment and conflict.

Instead, we need to again consider Alan Watts's paradox: only by accepting reality just as it is can we fully engage with that reality in the present moment, and then act spontaneously to generate positive change. Judgment by definition generates disengagement; we separate ourselves from the very situation we want to change.

*We disempower ourselves*
*each time we reject rather than accept*
*the reality of the moment.*
*As cowboys know from hard knocks,*
*nobody fights reality and wins.*

Consider a mother and her child. If the mother is continually judging and criticizing this child and putting the poor kid down for not somehow being better, does this actually help her child change for the better? Obviously, no. It's the same in a love relationship. Most couples don't accept each other just as they are. Instead they want the other person to change and become more pleasing and sexy and successful and so on.

But all such judgment kills love. According to my observation as a marriage counselor, chronic judgment and rejection wither and destroy a relationship. By not accepting people just as they are, we deny them love and the freedom to be fully themselves in the present moment, and to naturally grow in healthy directions. "I accept you just as you are" is the most loving thing you can say to your spouse.

The same dynamic occurs at work. To the extent that we criticize and otherwise reject the reality of a fellow worker, we inhibit instead of support that person's ability to change for the better. Love and acceptance generate compassion and positive change. Criticism and judgment block positive change. Fellow workers blossom when they're accepted and loved and valued. Companies become strong, creative, and resilient when there's mutual respect and compassion.

Similarly, calling Russia the "Evil Empire" was not an act of love toward the Russian people. And judging either Democrats or Republicans as somehow bad, stupid, irresponsible, greedy, or whatever is likewise not a mental projection that furthers the positive goals we all have.

*Meditation functions as an inner provocateur*
*promoting acceptance, compassion,*
*and love-based action*
*and stimulating a positive revolutionary process.*

If you meditate every waking minute of your life, holding these revolutionary Focus Phrases continually in mind as you interact with the world, then, according to the findings of the

PEAR research, you not only continually broadcast love and acceptance but also encourage ongoing positive change in the world.

I remember a bestselling self-help book published about forty years ago called *I'm OK, You're OK*. I'm saying the same thing — you're okay just the way you are right now. I'm okay just the way I am right now. The decisions we make and the actions we take represent the sum total of who we are, what we've been through, and what we hope to accomplish in the world. For me to judge your attitudes and actions negatively, as bad or stupid or irresponsible or greedy or whatever, seems entirely counterproductive.

All things considered, you're doing the best you can right now. And you need love and acceptance in order to flourish, not hatred and condemnation. So do I. So, shall we make a deal to accept each other just as we are, to respect each other and stop insisting on growth and change before granting acceptance and love?

Try this: bring to mind someone you know, anybody. Hold this person in your mind and heart a moment, then say to him or her: "I accept you just as you are."

Ah, what a relief! You feel a great flood of relaxation and joy when you realize you can accept others just as they are. They're fine! Let them be. They're not your responsibility. Let them off the judgment hook, and you set them free to flower and flourish. And at the same time, you set yourself free.

Every day, run through the list of people in your life, silently say to each of them, "I accept and love you just as you are," and experience the great release of compassion, energy, and spontaneous healing that you unleash. Say it. Do it. Give it a try right now, if you want:

*[Name of friend], I accept and love you just as you are.*

## REALITY ALWAYS WINS

Did you ever wonder why so many good people in the world yearn to improve nasty, unfair situations in the world, but seem to be so ineffective in generating positive change? The reason is that they are fighting reality, rather than participating in it. When I suggest that you accept the world just as it is in order to change it, I'm pointing out that you cannot change a situation unless you fully accept the fact that, right now, that situation exists exactly as it is. You cannot change this present moment. You can only embrace it. And then in the next moment, respond.

Not to accept a given situation or a particular person's attitude or behavior is to be in denial. And most of us are in denial, because the fear-based, reactive part of the mind is programmed to attack a danger, run away from that danger, or become unconscious to avoid the danger. There's no room for acceptance in a fear-based equation, because in such a case we let our anxiety about security drive our response to perceived danger.

Spiritual teachers have forever insisted that there's a fourth response: we have the power to raise our consciousness, fully perceive and accept a dangerous situation, and then bring to bear the power of love and compassionate engagement. For me, the fourth choice is the meditative choice. Only when we consciously take fear out of the equation do we become potent, positive agents for change.

This is the judo move that breaks the cycle of violence and

enables Spirit to enter a situation. In the next moment, when our hearts are open, anything can happen. As a world culture, I feel we must talk deeply and honestly and at length about this fourth choice. We must finally take Jesus and Buddha and other spiritual leaders seriously, and choose acceptance, compassion, and full spontaneous engagement as our modus operandi. Who knows, we might get hurt or lose money or even die in the process. We're going to die anyway at some point — and this heart-centered cause is truly worth living for.

It's time to celebrate the victory of love over fear: "I accept everyone I know, just as they are."

## ACCEPTANCE IN EXTREME SITUATIONS

The night before I wrote this chapter, an event occurred that dramatically demonstrates the power of the seventh Focus Phrase to transform anxiety and emotional suffering into a deep positive experience. My son, as usual, had driven to school and was due home around five o'clock. Six o'clock came and he wasn't home, nor had he called. Then seven o'clock came, darkness fell, and he still wasn't home. All parents go through the agony of waiting for their children when they're late and there's no word. Usually this is a time of high anxiety — one's mind goes crazy with negative imaginations. As I sat there looking out the window, waiting for my son's car lights to appear, I realized he could be in the hospital or worse; at any minute the phone could ring with terrible news.

I watched my mind playing all sorts of anxiety-projection fantasy games. My son had always been extremely punctual, and this had never happened before, so I could only assume that something dramatic had happened to him. Almost surely it would be a car accident. But there was nothing I could do, especially when I saw he hadn't taken his phone with him.

My mind raced, delivering worst-case scenarios and accident images. I caught myself slipping into an agonizingly anxious state, and then chose to say the Focus Phrases to help me not freak out as the minutes ticked by and my son failed to appear.

I watched my breaths come and go, used the first four Focus Phrases to bring myself fully into my body in the present moment, and said to myself, "I let go of all my stress and worries, and feel peaceful inside" and then "I accept this moment just as it is." This process took a couple of minutes, and I was actually a bit surprised to find how well it worked in such an extreme situation. Suddenly I actually felt good, because I felt connected in my heart with my son, wherever he was and whatever was happening to him. I realized that, regardless of what had happened, it had happened. There was nothing I could do to fight reality; all I could do was be open to the reality of the moment and be ready to respond from my heart and do what might be called for next.

If the phone rang and I found out he was in the hospital, I would rush there immediately to be with him. Even if I learned he'd been killed, that would be a reality I couldn't change, so I would accept it. That's just how life goes — tragedy does sometimes strike, and we must of necessity accept.

By surrendering to whatever had happened, I found myself watching my breathing, experiencing my presence in the room, and feeling relaxed and at peace as I sat there. For a moment, I actually felt guilty for feeling good, but then I realized that my becoming an emotional wreck would be of no value to my son, no matter what was happening in his life. So I continued to stay focused on the present moment and my breathing, said my Focus Phrases again and further quieted my mind, and just sat there, highly aware in the present moment, in deep communion with my son's presence and immersed in my love for him.

Time went by; no action. Seven thirty came and went. I continued to sit silently in the living room, looking out the window, now and then slipping into anxious worries and projections into the future, then pulling myself back to the present moment and saying to myself, "I accept whatever's happening."

Suddenly, there were car lights coming up our country drive, but I couldn't tell whether it was my son or the police coming to bring terrible news. The car lights flashed, then much to my relief the car pulled into our garage across the front lawn. Ah! It was our car; my son was okay, just delayed at school. I was elated!

I tell you this personal story as a real-life example of how the Focus Phrases can be used in the extreme situations that we all face now and then. I've also recounted this experience because it humbled me and reminded me that, no matter how much training we've had in mind management, in extreme situations we're all vulnerable to slipping back into old, anxious mental and emotional reactions.

I said before that I don't advocate striving to achieve a permanent state of enlightenment, in which a person is no longer vulnerable to human foibles. I find it important to remain fully human, rather than try to control my mind and emotions and transcend normal responses to situations. At the same time, as I found out while waiting for my son, the mind tools I discuss in this book do give us power to override fear-based reactions in favor of present-moment acceptance and trust.

The pragmatic reason for applying these mind tools in extreme situations is that getting caught up in anxious projections does no good and hinders a positive resolution to a difficult situation — freaking out is never a wise move. Full acceptance of the reality of the present moment keeps us in the optimum mental and emotional state for dealing successfully with whatever comes.

*Fear is a contraction; acceptance is an expansion.*
*Each moment, we choose one or the other.*

*"I accept the world just as it is right now."*

# CHAPTER EIGHT

# LOVE YOURSELF UNCONDITIONALLY

*The true spiritual path*
*requires no effort.*
*Simply open your heart*
*and love comes flowing in.*

—— THAKIN KUNG

The PEAR research demonstrated that when you focus your loving attention outward into the world you influence other people's hearts and minds in a positive way. But what happens when you take that same loving attention and aim it inward, toward your own center of being? This is the ongoing drama of meditation: What happens when you turn your loving focus 180 degrees and aim it at yourself?

You began this process of focusing inward with the first four Focus Phrases, which mobilized your perceptual powers. Now with the eighth Focus Phrase, you expand your focus to include conceptual and attitudinal dimensions of your relationship with yourself. To do this you'll need to once again remember that your ego decides where to focus your power of attention. So I say: "Hello again, ego! How do you feel about aiming your intent directly inward and saying the following Focus Phrase to yourself?"

*I honor and love myself just as I am.*

Do you in fact honor and love yourself just as you are? Tune in to your breathing right now for a few breaths, and then again say these elicitor words to yourself, to see how you respond emotionally to the very idea of loving yourself unconditionally: "I honor and love myself just as I am."

## SEEKING ABSOLUTION

Love in all cultures of this world is forever sacrosanct. All human beings experience the feeling of love, religions regard love as the primary quality of God, and families are held together by the power of love. All you need is love. Love is all there is. Love one another.

But we tend to do just the opposite, especially in our relationship with ourselves. Rather than loving ourselves unconditionally, we tend to judge ourselves as unworthy of even our own love. This eighth Focus Phrase insists that we nurture unconditional love for ourselves right now.

*We can't love others*
*more than we love ourselves —*
*so it's our inherent duty*

*to first learn to love ourselves*
*so that we can love others more.*

When I was attending seminary back in the 1970s, I spent two afternoons a week for almost a year working at San Quentin prison with a group of fourteen lifers, all of whom had murdered at least one person. I still remember moving through all those security locks and then getting locked up myself in a room with these fourteen murderers and two guards with machine guns. *Clang* would go the metal door, and then there we were. This seemed like one hell of a way to begin my work as a pastoral psychologist, but in retrospect I wouldn't have given it up for anything.

In the beginning I was afraid of these fourteen men, and I judged them to the hilt. But, step-by-step, as I allowed these human beings to tell their life stories, I shifted from judging them to understanding them. And after three or four months, I reached the point where a line from a folk song popular at the time best expressed my emerging feelings: "There but for fortune go you and I."

Five of these men were definitely out-and-out psychopaths who simply felt nothing one way or another about what they'd done — in early childhood all of them had been tortured and abused to the point that they were hopelessly damaged. The others felt a gamut of emotions and were in the process of understanding and, I hope, forgiving themselves and finding some sort of inner absolution and spiritual peace. At the time, born-again religious fervor was rampant in San Quentin; rather than forgiving themselves for what they'd done, prisoners were encouraged to ask God and Jesus to forgive them. Somehow this didn't seem to work for the prisoners in my group. These nine men had come to realize that no one else, not even God, could forgive them if they couldn't forgive themselves first.

As a therapist, I have found this is true of all of us. The great blockage between our inner selves and the healing power of Spirit inflow is our ego's self-judgment. One way or another, we must reach the point where we fully accept who we are and what we've done, and then forgive ourselves, before love can flow into our hearts and make us whole. You cannot change the past. All you can do is accept whatever happened, and choose to let spiritual love flow in. Then you can move on. This is the very nature of human reality.

In most cases, inner healing does not require traditional therapy. You simply need to accept and let go of the past, generate a clear intent to honor and love yourself just as you are — and state this intent over and over again. Each time you say to yourself the eighth Focus Phrase, you focus your attention precisely on accepting and loving yourself. And the more often you do so, the farther you will move in this direction. "I honor and love myself just as I am."

## SET YOURSELF FREE

Is there any reason not to honor and love yourself just as you are right now? I remember sitting many times under the oak trees in Ojai, or in an auditorium in Europe or elsewhere, and listening to Krishnamurti as he guided us patiently through a clear logical analysis of why self-judgment is an entirely unnecessary function of the human mind, and why self-love is essential to spiritual health and fulfillment.

He would point out that many religious leaders had done their best to convince us that we are hopeless sinners who can be made whole only by the intercession of an external God or occult power. He would state emphatically that this particular "you're born a hopeless sinner" belief was not a clear reflection of reality, and that accepting such a priestly dictum was spiritual suicide. Here is one of his more acerbic statements:

> *Religion is the frozen thought of man*
> *out of which they build temples.*
> *It is no measure of health*
> *to be well adjusted to*
> *a sick belief system.*

Perhaps this is an extreme statement. Krishnamurti considered belief in any religious dictum unwise. But it does seem wrong that people find it difficult to honor and love themselves unconditionally because they've been programmed with religious attitudes that make them chronic prisoners of their own self-judgment.

As a psychologist, I too am obliged to state the facts as I see them, even if doing so alienates members of the religious right. The root assumption of Christianity, after all, is that we are all born utterly hopeless sinners because of a negative choice made by our first ancestors. As I was taught emphatically at seminary, Christian theology is clear that unredeemed human nature is evil, and that we can do absolutely nothing about this evilness on our own. We must surrender our souls to a religious institution claiming that, through a theological concept called Jesus Christ, it has the power to absolve us of our sins and make us pure.

As long as we believe this radical negative judgment of our human souls, we remain victims of this belief and relinquish the capacity to honor and love ourselves just as we are. After all, how can we love ourselves if our very nature is utterly degraded, sinful, evil, and depraved?

I realize that, with this eighth Focus Phrase, I'm again crying out for revolution. But I see no reason not to. Even the growing minority of citizens of our culture who weren't formally raised as Christians were imprinted with the underlying Christian belief that we're somehow no good and must chronically struggle to make ourselves better. Once we see this situation clearly, each of us must choose whether to believe a religious dictum that judges us as inherently evil, or to rise up and, over and over again, declare our freedom from that belief — and state our new vision of love beyond all religious indictments.

Again, this is my own opinion based on subjective inquiry into the subject. I encourage you to take action yourself — see how it feels to you to say these elicitor words. Let them resonate deep in your heart, and be open to a new experience:

*I honor and love myself just as I am.*

## THE POWER OF ACCEPTANCE

When I moved to West Berlin in the 1980s, as a spiritually focused psychologist who integrated the emotional-healing techniques of Wilhelm Reich with Krishnamurti's pragmatic approach to secular meditation, an elderly man high up in German politics came to me in a hush of privacy and asked if I would take him on as a client. I soon found out that he had been a powerful Nazi who had managed to avoid prosecution after the war. Now, forty years later, he was seeking inner absolution for what he had done.

Within weeks, six other ex-Nazis came to me on his rec-ommendation. As a young American therapist with a spiritual bent, I found myself seriously in over my head. Luckily, while studying at Princeton I'd met a remarkable therapist, named Carl Rogers, who created the therapy technique that later came to be called Rogerian therapy. I distinctly remember a demon-stration that Carl gave of his technique to a group of about two hundred students in a lecture hall at Princeton. He walked out onto the stage, sat in a chair facing the audience, and for fifty-five minutes simply sat there attentively, focused on us with empathy — but not saying or doing anything at all. Then he stood up, nodded, and walked off the stage.

Carl's therapy technique was to simply listen to a client with full attention and zero expectations, feeling unconditional acceptance and love — period. He didn't analyze, he didn't ad-vise, he didn't ask questions or offer behavioral-modification techniques. And he certainly didn't recommend medication or religious commitment. All he did was listen without judgment, with openhearted empathy and acceptance.

However difficult this approach might be for me personally, I decided this was the best way to deal with my seven ex-Nazis. I simply listened to them without judging them as they poured their hearts out to me. My one request was that they stay aware of their breathing as much as possible, all through a session.

I did two-hour sessions with each of them twice a week. Each session began with a fifteen-minute massage, then I sat quietly with them and let them express themselves. Whenever emotions rose to the surface, I used Reich's special release tech-niques to help the emotions come fully out and be discharged. And at the end of the session, I sat in meditation with the client for around twenty minutes. (I still consider this an ideal ther-apy structure, although I no longer do therapy.)

The results with these old men amazed me. They were all top dogs in German business or the government, solidly established in the ruling social and economic circles — and yet they were ready to finally let down their guards. Three of these men never did manage to fully accept and love themselves just as they were, but the other four did.

By looking honestly at their memories, attitudes, emotions, and reactions over and over again, they began to re-experience and then let go of their self-judgment and the judgment of others. Somewhere in the therapy/inquiry process, as I taught them basic meditation techniques to practice at home, they began to open their hearts and experience that amazing spark of spiritual love that, in the end, is the only healing balm that overcomes self-judgment and allows us to forgive ourselves… and see ourselves for who we really are.

*When negative attitudes and emotions*
*chronically knock us out of balance,*
*we naturally seek homeostasis.*
*There exists a natural emotional*
*and attitudinal healing process*
*that we all can activate.*
*Meditation is a structured way*
*to encourage homeostasis to*
*regularly kick into gear.*

## WHAT ARE WE AFRAID OF?

Here's the question: what would happen if you actually did love yourself just as you are? Most people seem to be downright afraid of doing this. What is this fear? Beyond the Christian programming that tells us we are born hopeless sinners, there's something else going on here, and we need to look right into the heart of it.

Many of us seem to be afraid that, if we relax and accept ourselves with all our shortcomings, we'll fail to suceed and survive. Here we are again, looking at the fear of death as a driver of our lives. Our society compels us to perpetually try to improve ourselves, and the constant need to achieve is a plague on our society. We all push our kids to be superachievers at the top of the class, even though this means that most of them end up feeling like underachievers. This leads to the loss of self-acceptance, and in turn makes them feel miserable, unworthy, and depressed as adults.

It's crazy, really, to push children as we do, simply out of fear. The majority of people in our culture feel like failures in life because they didn't meet the impossible expectations of their parents and teachers.

So we have great difficulty accepting ourselves just as we are, because we're afraid that who we are right now isn't good enough. Even tentatively entertaining the thought of accepting ourselves as we are can feel threatening. The New Age movement, built on the premise that we are not okay as we are but must constantly work to improve ourselves on all levels, is a prominent example.

Look at this closely: we have an ingrained fear that, if we decide to honor and love ourselves just as we are, we'll lose our motivation for chronically pushing ourselves to get ahead in life. And we deeply fear losing this motivation. We worship success and advancement — and we judge the present moment itself as not good enough. But is this true?

*Aren't we capable of enjoying life just as it is right now?*
*Must we make things better before*
*we can ease up and enjoy ourselves?*

The eighth Focus Phrase is specifically designed to deactivate that "I'm not good enough" fear that keeps you from loving yourself just as you are. When you don't love yourself just as you are, life is hell. If you do love yourself just as you are, life is good. So let's apply reason, and choose to enjoy this moment as perfectly adequate, and ourselves as perfectly adequate as well.

## THE VOICE OF REASON

Krishnamurti insisted that we must inquire deeply into the issues that underlie human suffering, and identify the beliefs that must be put aside so we can embrace the present moment. Here's what he said during a talk I attended in Ojai in 1966:

> To ask the right question demands a great deal of intelligence and sensitivity. Here is a fundamental question: is life a torture? It is, as it is usually lived; man has lived in this torture centuries upon centuries, from ancient history to the present day, in agony, in despair, in sorrow; and he doesn't find a way out of it. Therefore he invents gods, churches, all the rituals, and all that nonsense, or he escapes in different ways.
>
> What we are trying to do during these discussions and talks is to see if we cannot radically bring about a transformation of the mind, not accept things as they are, nor revolt against them. You must understand the situation, go into it, examine it — give your heart and

your mind with everything that you have to find out a way of living differently. That depends on you, and not on someone else, because in this there is no teacher, no pupil, no leader, no guru; there is no Master, no Savior. You yourself are the teacher and the pupil; you are the Master; you are the leader; you are everything. To understand is to transform what is.

Krishnamurti suggested that we put aside all beliefs and simply look at the reality of the situation. Why do we suffer emotionally? How do our minds generate chronic anxiety and the hostility and chaos that emerge from anxiety? And most important, how can we transform our minds so that we no longer suffer, but instead enjoy each new moment free of conflict and fear?

My particular answer, which has evolved over the years, is the set of Focus Phrases I'm teaching you. Predictably, they aim your attention beyond programmed beliefs and worries, at a deeper sense of truth and reality. Are you lovable or not? Are you okay just as you are or not? I say you are, but don't take my word for it. Let the eighth Focus Phrase gently and accurately aim your attention — and discover for yourself the truth inside you: "I honor and love myself just as I am."

## ARE YOU WORTHY?

With a Krishnamurti-like eye for truth, let's look at the general assumption that you are not perfectly okay just as you are. Using your unique understanding of the word *God*, consider the following statements:

- God (or whatever name you call God) created this universe; I am part of this universe; therefore I am God's creation.
- I am a personal expression of the Creator, and every breath I breathe is a gift from God.
- I am the eyes and ears of God; whatever I experience is experienced by the infinite Spirit.
- I naturally have the creative spark of Spirit inside me, animating my existence each moment.
- My very nature is spiritual. When I look directly at the core of my being, I find I am not a weird, soulless, demonic creature devoid of spiritual insight and expression. I am a personal expression of the Creator.

If indeed you are inextricably connected with Spirit, if you are a manifestation of God's infinite love and wisdom, then why do you sit around knocking yourself over the head with negative beliefs that claim just the opposite?

I think it's time for me to make a big confession. A lot of people get upset when I make this confession, but I do my best to practice what I preach, and this leads me inexorably to the following confession: I am no longer trying to improve myself. I'm not trying to become more spiritual. I don't care at all about becoming enlightened. I feel in my heart that I'm okay just as I am. Nothing needs to change in order for me to honor and love myself unconditionally. I've given up the struggle for perfection. I feel perfectly fine just as I am. Take it or leave it — this is me.

I must say it's a remarkable relief to have arrived at this point where I feel okay about myself, and experience no pressure to do anything at all to improve who I am deep down. The feeling of honoring and loving myself just as I am is so wonderful that I'm entirely satisfied.

Nowhere to go, nothing to do. This, for me, is what inner peace is all about. "I honor and love myself just as I am."

## WHY THE "HONOR" PART?

Good question — why do we have to bring honor into this equation? Isn't love enough? I can't tell you why honor is essential, at an intellectual level, to this Focus Phrase. All I can say is that, if it's left out, the power of this Focus Phrase becomes greatly reduced for most people.

The word *honor* is an elicitor term that naturally evokes a deep response in us. Honor is about respect and equality. Mutual respect and honoring one another's integrity is a shared understanding that supports and nurtures human relationship. Honor and love together create a unified whole, and prompt the shift from self-judgment to self-acceptance.

When we bring the term *honor* into this Focus Phrase, the term *love* becomes more clearly defined and empowered. Once again, remember that it's your ego saying, "I honor and love myself just as I am." Somehow the word *honor* clarifies, to the judgmental ego, exactly what this new relationship with oneself is about. To the ego, honor is important.

Again, please experiment and discover for yourself the power of these elicitor words. During the next weeks say this Focus Phrase often to yourself and stay open to your reactions and insights in response to the inner act of honoring and loving yourself.

Several questions may help you as contemplate the eighth Focus Phrase:

1. How would your life change if you decided to love and accept yourself just as you are?

2. Are you a hopeless sinner, or are you a perfect creation of God?

3. Is there anything about you that you feel you must change before you can honor and love yourself just as you are?

4. How would you feel in your heart if you were to love yourself unconditionally?

*Pause and Reflect*

## ALAN'S PARADOX FULFILLED

Throughout this chapter I've been talking about letting go of future goals of trying to make yourself better and, instead, accepting yourself as perfectly okay in the present moment. Taking this leap of faith offers a remarkable payoff — you will finally feel truly good in your heart about both yourself and the world around you.

As I think you'll agree, until you truly love yourself, you cannot fully love another person. As soon as you allow love for yourself to live in your heart, your love for others will increase, flow outward, and flourish. This is reason enough to make the eighth Focus Phrase a pivotal point of the rest of your life.

But there's more — in the middle of this Focus Phrase exists a remarkable, uplifting paradox. The entire Uplift meditation process is characterized by this paradox, in the Alan Watts, Zen-based tradition. And once again, the paradox is this: as you accept yourself just as you are, love floods into the present moment and provokes positive change in you.

We come to the primary difference between trying to manipulate our lives, and surrendering to and participating in the eternal change that's always happening in the present moment. As the Taoist tradition of China so clearly expresses, change is the only constant. And when we accept ourselves and the world as perfect in this moment, we set ourselves free to participate in this moment as it changes and evolves into the next moment.

Once again, we're back to what I consider an irrefutable universal human truth:

- Only when we stop judging, and hold love rather than fear in our hearts, do we enable Spirit to flow into our personal lives.
- Only in the emerging present moment do God's guidance and power influence our evolution.
- Only when we stop trying to improve ourselves do we spontaneously transform our presence as spiritual beings.

What I'm talking about here is the cutting edge of my own current spiritual evolution, the underlying dynamic of the interaction between God the Creator and us the created.

How does God interact with our physical world? According to traditional religions, God actually interfered with historic situations, punishing tribes or blessing them, deciding who would win wars and who would lose. But I have never experienced the presence of a God who takes sides in personal or social situations, who answers the prayers of one side and dumps on the other side.

However, I have grown increasingly aware over the years that when human beings open their hearts and allow Spirit to inflow they become living vehicles and personal expressions of the infinite creative force that is our universe's Source.

*When we open our hearts to Spirit*
*and our minds to inspiration,*
*our thoughts and hearts become guided*
*by a higher wisdom and power.*
*This is always our choice.*
*Hell is when we are closed to higher guidance.*
*Heaven on earth is when we are open.*
*Love is the medium.*
*What a choice!*

The middle four Focus Phrases as a unit will help you open emotionally. They gently and predictably awaken emotional clarity, attitudinal healing, and unconditional love, so that you're fully prepared to open and receive whatever insight, inspiration, compassion, and empowerment the universe is bringing to you right now.

Please use the first eight Focus Phrases as a rapid daily, or even hourly, process to bring yourself to the point where you're ready and open to receive. Make sure you clear the way in your own psyche, step-by-step, so that you respond less from anxiety and more from the heart.

Then, when you go on and activate the ninth and tenth Focus Phrases, you'll be able to naturally receive unique new insights and enter into communion with the divine. This preparation takes only a couple of minutes when you become adept at it, and it's essential for the success of the next Focus Phrases.

To end this chapter, let's move through the following eight-step preparation for opening to receive spiritual flow:

*I choose to enjoy this moment.*

*I feel the air flowing in and out of my nose.*

*I also feel the movements in my chest and belly as I breathe.*

*I'm aware of my whole body at once, here in this present moment.*

*I am ready to experience the feelings in my heart.*

*I let go of all my stress and worries and feel peaceful inside.*

*I accept everyone I know, just as they are.*

*I honor and love myself just as I am.*

# CHAPTER NINE

# OPEN...AND RECEIVE

*When the individual mind*
*touches the Universal Mind*
*it receives all that it requires.*

*In order to receive guidance*
*the receiver must be in tune*
*with the transmitter.*
*Then you will be ready to receive*
*the information or inspiration or wisdom*
*necessary for the development of your purpose.*

— CHARLES HAANEL

We now leave the emotional-clearing phase and arrive at the point where there's truly nothing to do, nowhere to go — and all things are possible. Your mind is quiet, you're at peace in your heart and with the world, in love mode rather than fear mode, ready to open wide your heart and soul and move into a spiritually receptive state of consciousness.

In review, here is the eight-step progression you make each time you approach the ninth Focus Phrase:

1. Choose to enjoy this moment
2. Refresh your breath link
3. Wake up your solar plexus

4.  Regain whole-body presence
5.  Experience your heart
6.  Move beyond anxiety
7.  Accept everyone right now
8.  Love yourself unconditionally

The first eight Focus Phrases induce a state of consciousness that allows you to feel safe and at least somewhat free of negative programming and old emotional contractions. Now it's time to actively state your intent to further open your heart, mind, and soul into full receptive mode.

The ninth Focus Phrase is utterly simple and immensely powerful:

*I am open to receive.*

## NO EXPECTATIONS

You are not expected to suddenly and fully open up the first time you say this Focus Phrase. All of life is a progression, and at each moment you are spontaneously evolving and growing. What you're looking for here isn't a sudden "total enlightenment" experience. You're simply encouraging yourself to experience an effortless movement in the direction of your infinite God nature.

As mentioned earlier, I'm not an advocate of traditional forms of enlightenment. I no longer hunger to be totally emancipated from all my human quirks and quandaries. I love being a human being, just as I am right now, and I'm leaving the potential enlightenment stuff for after I die. Many spiritual folk disagree with me on this, and that's fine. But I do want to point out again that, as long as we are dissatisfied with ourselves just as we are, as long as we're striving toward an ideal that we hope to reach in the future, we're not fully living in the present moment. Each moment we focus on the future goal of becoming enlightened, we're absent from the natural spiritual experience that comes to us only here and now.

When you say to yourself, "I am open to receive," it's important to be open to what you truly need to receive right now. All ego anticipation must be put aside so that genuine inspiration, beyond ego desires and imaginations, can come to you.

In my experience, when it comes to what we need right here, right now, we can never outguess God. Ego by definition is a limited mental function that can take past experience and generate lofty imaginations about what we might receive in meditation. But every time we try to qualify what we want to receive, we limit the power of Spirit to bring us anything beyond what our ego imagines.

The ninth Focus Phrase is a leap of faith when approached without ego expectations. When we move beyond words, concepts, beliefs, and expectations, we open ourselves to the infinite potential of Spirit flowing into our lives.

How do you feel about taking this leap? Each time you come to this Focus Phrase and say to yourself, "I am open to receive," you actively open usually closed doors and welcome the touch of God on your personal awareness. That's an amazing thing to do; it's the ultimate step in leading your horse to water. Now it's time to drink: "I am open to receive."

## TRUSTING THE INFLOW

Right about here, many people who were brought up in the Christian tradition start jumping up and down and shouting at me. How on earth could I encourage people to open their hearts and minds willy-nilly to whatever esoteric forces might be out there ready to grab their souls and pull them into eternal oblivion?

I remember struggling with this fear myself as a teenager. I was taught that a devil exists out there, an evil force beyond the control of God or Christ, a horrendous anti-God power that is invisible and yet everywhere — like God, only the opposite of God. In Christian theology, this evil force is always trying to find a way to slip into our minds, grab our souls, and drag us down into eternal hellfire.

What an amazing thing to program into the minds of children. In one of my more radical books, *Jesus for the Rest of Us*, I went so far as to call this programming "psychological child abuse." So many people suffer greatly because they were programmed with this horrendous "scare flick" occult belief.

Programming people to fear the inflow of hell and damnation whenever they open their hearts in trust during meditation is an ideal psychological technique for limiting independent spiritual discovery, and for instilling abject fear in the populace so they can be easily manipulated. But this is not a kind or fair or loving thing to do, to anyone.

So unavoidably, yes, we come to this point in the Uplift meditation where I suggest you do something that'd make any God-fearing Puritan run screaming into the forest to avoid: I recommend that you choose to throw away all fear of an evil force in the universe, and open your heart in total trust and love, so that you receive direct spiritual flow untainted by programmed beliefs.

I can wholeheartedly recommend doing this because I've

been looking all my life for even the slightest sign of an evil force in the universe, and except for certain psychotic aberrations in mentally ill people, I have yet to encounter this evil force. Yes, it's true that a great many people throughout the world sometimes behave in an insane manner and do atrocious things to themselves and others — and sometimes appear to be participating in an evil esoteric conspiracy. Furthermore, mob psychology has shown us that even normal people can get caught up in weird beliefs and do horrendous things. But the persistent presence of temporary or permanent human psychosis is not proof of an occult evil force in the universe.

It's possible that you disagree with me on this point, and that's fine. All I ask is that you use the ninth Focus Phrase to explore the reality of the experience that comes to you in this meditative process.

## GOD'S REALITY SHOW

Let's examine again the vast difference between a belief (such as a belief in the devil) and a meditative experience. When your thinking mind becomes quiet during the first phase of the Uplift meditation, all imaginations about the devil naturally fade away. You are simply present in the here and now, aware and alert, and focused on your spiritual core.

Please notice that the first eight Focus Phrases are very important in directing your attention to spiritual, as opposed to theological, realms of consciousness. Even if there were a devil waiting to grab your soul when you quiet your mind and open to receive, the Uplift process would protect you from psychic danger. Why? Because you are not a passive participant in this meditation. You actively determine the direction of your attention's focus each time you open to receive.

Meditation as we're approaching it here is a responsible,

mature act. You're not choosing to focus on negative, fear-based dimensions that do or do not exist. You are purposefully and clearly focusing your "receive mode" attention toward the true spiritual depths of your being.

Once you've aligned yourself in this spiritual direction, you've made it absolutely clear that you have zero intent to focus on negative occult beliefs and imaginations. Of course, if for some reason you choose to believe in a world where there is a devil, you can surely create in your mind an imaginary experience of that world. But please recognize a figment of your mind's creation, as opposed to a reality beyond that imagination.

One of the great effects of meditation (as taught clearly in the "insight meditation" of Buddhist tradition) is that you come to develop a strong, clear sense of what is real, as opposed to what you've conjured. The first eight Focus Phrases actively put aside your ego imaginations, as you enter into the reality show that God's putting on. This is a show well worth watching and learning from. Here's your ticket:

*I am open to receive.*

## VARIATIONS ON THE INFLOW THEME

Feel free to sometimes vary the wording of the ninth Focus Phrase to reflect what is most important to you at the moment. For instance, sometimes I find myself saying, "My heart is open to receive love and peace." Or I say, "I am open to receive God's healing touch." At other times I might say, "I'm open to receive guidance and insight." I might even find myself saying, "I am open to receive financial inflow." Or simply: "I'm open."

Choose any variation that feels right for you at the moment. And remember that it's not necessary to believe in God or any particular notion of spiritual inflow and empowerment in order for the Focus Phrases to affect your life. The point is that you're tapping into reality, not some belief about reality. Even at a purely psychological level, it's an amazing experience to feel open rather than habitually closed. In your dealings with other people, the economic system, your immune system, and other systems, to be open to receive, rather than closed off from the world, is a powerfully enabling posture.

So often in relationships, we try to love one another even though our hearts are habitually contracted and not open to receive. As I discussed in depth in *Let Love Find You*, there's no point in seeking a fulfilling relationship if you don't first say the ninth Focus Phrase to yourself over and over and experience the progressive opening of your heart.

Here's the basic fact: until you reach the point where you trust other people and the universe enough to be receptive, you're probably going to feel lonely, depressed, and anxious a great deal of the time. In saying the earlier Focus Phrases, you choose to let go of your anxieties and your judgments. With this new Focus Phrase you actively begin to experience trust, acceptance, compassion, and faith.

## A NEW PRAYER

I grew up in a Christian prayer tradition that was mainly focused on asking God to do things for me and for people I loved: "Please, God, hear my prayer and do such and such." I no longer experience a God who does specific favors for me or others simply because I ask him to. I cannot imagine a God who plays favorites because of prayer petitions. The old type of prayer, no matter how lovingly motivated, just doesn't work for me anymore.

Spirit doesn't force its way into our hearts. Whether we accept it is always our choice. But spiritual help and guidance are always available, eager to flow in when we open up. And to the extent that we welcome Spirit and love into our personal lives, we can also choose to allow love and inspiration to flow outward from our centers and into the hearts of others. In this entirely unaggressive way, Spirit does directly touch the outside world and participate in the outcome of historic events — through us!

In the traditional form of prayer that I was taught, I remained mostly in broadcast mode rather than receive mode, talking nonstop to my concept of God, asking him to intercede in the world and bring about what I wanted to have happen. I was in essence asking God to play favorites, trying to manipulate him into manipulating the physical world. "Dear God, please make things go the way my fearful ego wants them to."

As demonstrated in the PEAR studies at Princeton, meditative prayer expresses a more mature act of the heart. It entails the subtle but realistic involvement of spiritual flow into everyday life, through our focused attention.

*Meditative prayer uses your personal consciousness*
*to channel the universal power of love,*
*harmony, and healing intent*
*into the world.*

## LETTING LOVE DO IT

Meditative prayer is about listening, receiving, and respond-ing. The assumption underlying it is that the universe is God's creation and is continually unfolding as it should. So, logically, when we participate in this deeper unfolding we don't tell God what to do, but choose to receive and broadcast an inspired consciousness as we radiate a positive spiritual presence into the world.

It's essential to keep fearful projections of the ego mind quiet throughout the process. This is accomplished first by staying aware of your breathing and your whole-body pres-ence. Sometimes, as mentioned before, when you say the sev-enth Focus Phrase, "I accept everyone I know, just as they are," you will feel the natural desire to send love and acceptance into the world. Likewise, with the ninth Focus Phrase (I am open to receive), you will often find yourself spontaneously wanting to also focus on giving, and as you become aware of a particular friend, loved one, or colleague, your heart will open up to this person. You'll experience a natural outflow of the same spiri-tual love, healing, and insight that you're in the process of re-ceiving.

All you need to do is allow this person's presence to be-come clear and strong within you. Then focus loving attention, total acceptance, and openhearted compassion toward this per-son's presence in the here and now. In this way, you can chan-nel spiritual love and energy into the world and other people's hearts without manipulating them or the deeper flow of the present moment in history.

There's also another, more extreme giving-loving-accepting experience that might come to you. Sometimes I surprise my-self by focusing suddenly on a nasty world leader, terrorist, criminal, or other negative presence or situation, and allow the bright spiritual feelings that have flowed into my heart to flow out to this person or situation. This aims love exactly where it's most needed, where the pain and craziness are most acute in the world. The PEAR studies indicate that we can use our personal attention to influence the world, and meditative prayer expresses this radical type of action.

Just be sure you don't slip back into an old habit of prayer and think you "should" be doing something to help others around you. In my understanding, the giving mode must come spontaneously, as your heart's natural response to receiving spiritual love, insight, and power.

And so, to end this chapter, you might want to relax, choose to enjoy this moment, tune in to your breathing and your heart, and let go of worries and judgments. Then, without any expectations, see what experience comes to you as you stay aware of your breathing and hold the ninth Focus Phrase gently and clearly in your mind:

*I am open to receive.*

CHAPTER TEN

# MERGE WITH YOUR SOURCE

*Get beyond the mind*
*and beyond time*
*and enter into eternal silence*
*which is eternal life.*

*Once you have tasted that life*
*your whole existence*
*becomes a celebration.*

— OSHO

We are ready to delve into the deepest Focus Phrase of this meditation program. And even at the risk of presenting myself in what some might call a radical or negative light, I'd like to share with you an experience that came to me at the climax of one of the most extreme periods of my life. I do so because the experience led me into an awakening that has strongly influenced my life ever since. In it, I pushed my limits so intensely that I suddenly came face-to-face, whether I wanted to or not, with the Source, the origin of my life force.

My hope, in developing and teaching the new meditation process I present in this book, is that you won't have to push your own limits so far in order to open up and experience your connection with the Source.

I'd grown up in a conservative, religious, and, in retrospect, anxious and judgmental family and cultural environment. In the 1960s, I'd broken free and explored various avenues for psychological and spiritual healing and awakening. But as I entered my early thirties I still hadn't healed a lot of my ingrained fears and inhibitions. Instead I'd mostly put aside my wild spiritual-exploration days and become a successful emotional-release therapist in San Luis Obispo. I was living in a beautiful house, most of which my brother and I had built with our own hands, and I owned twenty acres of magnificent open country up in the hills. My wife at the time was content with our material situation, and my son from an earlier marriage was living with us. No longer living on the edge, I'd settled into routines of material security and success and seemed to be living the good life.

But deep down spiritually, I was quietly going crazy, having stepped off the heart path and let go of my earlier sense of connectedness with my center. I became seriously judgmental about the materialistic Yuppie trends I'd temporarily embraced, and felt discouraged because few of my therapy clients wanted to delve seriously into the new emotional-release techniques I'd been developing.

Hungering more and more intensely for whatever was missing from my inner life, I started pulling back from my cozy secure world and made choices that distanced me from my wife and friends. I felt almost compulsively determined to break free once and for all from my religious and cultural conditioning and inherited emotional contractions. I began to once again listen to the guidance of my inner voice, and as I became openly averse to what I considered the plastic consumer culture of California, I experienced the disintegration of my second marriage.

I sent my son to live with his mom for a year, and I left my home and practice. Soon I was living an entirely new life in a very different culture, having driven my Volkswagen camper all the way to Central America, and then settled into a cottage on the edge of the native Mayan culture at a highland lake called Lago Atitlán, in Guatemala. I had enough money to live for at least a year on a low budget, and for several months I retreated from everyone and everything, spending my days and nights alone in a solitary, quasi-meditative routine.

·I wasn't especially spiritually alert during those quiet months of retreat, but something important was relaxing and letting go. I played my guitar for hours on end and wrote a whole bunch of introspective songs. I tuned in to the peaceful pace and ancient routines of the native Mayans living communal lives, at a subsistence level, around the lake, and began to respond to their inclusiveness and heart connectedness, which I hadn't felt since Granny had died many years earlier. Something in me was healing. Deep down, though, part of me still felt wounded and lost.

## JOINING THE OTHER SIDE

One day, out of the blue, I felt compelled or guided — call it what you will — to take the mail boat twenty miles across the lake to explore the rugged mountain wilderness where the ancient Indian culture still prevailed, and where revolutionaries were still highly active. I remember feeling myself come alive with raw anticipation, and enjoyed the adventuresome spring in my gait as the little boat docked at the wooden pier in Santiago Atitlán, and I walked past native fishing *cayucos* and women wearing traditional *wipiles* with babies strapped to their backs.

In just a few days, while I stayed at a local hostel, my mind shifted, becoming slower, more alert and sensitive. Then one morning while out hiking, I encountered and fell headlong into an intense and dangerous love affair with a young Mayan woman who led a renegade band of fighters against Guatemala's military regime. Mahalena was uniquely beautiful. One-quarter German and possessing a complex background, she woke up a strong "noble outlaw" feeling inside me.

For several months I thought I'd finally found a truly worthwhile cause and pristine culture to join — and Mahalena seemed to be the lover I'd been seeking all my life. She was young, brave, mystically deep, and totally dedicated to defending the freedom of her native community. After she brought me into her small gang, I set to work writing in longhand what I hoped would be an intense, true tale of good versus evil.

We lived in caves and huts on the volcanic slopes of the towering Atitlán crater. It was an exhilarating as well as strenuous and dangerous life. I began to understand the hopes and beliefs and occult practices of that tribe, and worked to transform their story into a great novel that would wake the world to the ongoing genocidal atrocities of the Guatemalan government. Those were the best and worst of times, as new physical, emotional, and mystic experiences provoked new awakenings in me and shattered many of my personal and cultural illusions.

Mahalena was an inspired and inspiring human being. I've since written several novels about her and this period of my life (*Powerpoint*; *The Vision Mehee*), each time trying to delve deeper into the truth of her and her people and their almost mythic story. But to be honest, at some point I seriously lost my center. My ego took over and I began to think that my own lofty view was the only view, and that my whole civilization up north was bad and wrong and evil.

I can see now that I was in over my head, caught up in someone else's battle and romanticizing the whole thing, including my own role and purpose. I also began arguing with the old native *brujo* (shaman) of the group, and tried to dominate Mahalena as well. Then one day it all exploded.

That morning, Mahalena left me to focus on my writing, as usual, and went off with her little gang — and was shot and killed by government troops. I heard the devastating news and escaped back to the tourist side of the lake, but with a curse by the local *brujo* on my head to prevent me from leaving the lake alive, because I'd learned too much of the tribe's occult tradition. For some reason the old man also blamed me for Mahalena's death. Within hours of arriving on the safe side of the lake and settling into a tiny rental cottage, I was laid low by a radical physical condition that nearly did take my life.

## BEHOLD THE LIFE FORCE

My experience during the next eight days while I was flat on my back in Panahachel was one of progressive, and finally abject, surrender. I'd left my culture and shaken the dust of California from my boots, intending never to return. I had judged everything up north as seriously unacceptable, and had judged myself as unacceptable too. But the joke was on me — I found out the hard way that a man can't live long when disconnected from himself and his roots. I was dying.

The only doctor on that side of the lake was a drunk who came and saw me once and never showed up again. Because of the *brujo*'s curse — or not, who can say — I'd contracted hepatitis from drinking the water. My eyes turned yellow, my liver swelled, and my appetite disappeared. Even more seriously, I was also possessed by some devastating parasites that were busy gobbling up my insides and further reducing my life force.

But mostly I'd just reached the end of my tether spiritually. I was shattered by the violent death of the woman I loved, and I was dying along with her. There was, however, a spiritual lining. For three days, toward the end, I let go of my fear of death. I became utterly at peace inside my heart, my ego surrendered and seemingly disappeared, and I went for several days without thinking hardly a thought.

I'd finally attained the meditative state of consciousness I'd hungered for so intensely during my earlier years. But the price for this inner clarity seemed, to put it mildly, quite high.

A young Indian girl came by twice a day from the native hut next door and brought me fruit and Coca-Cola. She was like an angel, and was maybe ten years old. She simply sat there on the patio beside my sleeping mat for perhaps half an hour each morning. She seemed to fully accept whatever was happening to me; the Indians in that village lived with death as much as they did with life.

But then one day she didn't come. I lay there unmoving hour after hour, my breaths coming and going all on their own. Then at some point I began to feel the most intense sensation in my toes and the soles of my feet. I experienced what I can only describe as my life force beginning to unravel, counterclockwise, a sensation that started in my feet and, over the next hour or so, moved slowly up into my knees and then my thighs.

All of a sudden, as my knees started tingling and then became numb, I knew viscerally that my death was imminent. On a level far beyond that of my ego, I had given up maintaining my existence. And right at that moment, when I knew that I was dying and had surrendered totally, something opened deep down in my heart and solar plexus, and I could vividly hear and see and feel and smell and otherwise experience the presence of Spirit flowing into my body. As if I'd been directly plugged into the Source socket, I felt inexorably connected with my Creator.

There's no way really to talk about that experience — but I can tell you one thing: at that moment, emerging like lava from the core of my being, in response to my mortal unwinding I heard my own voice shouting loud and clear: "No — I don't want to die!"

Exactly at that moment, I felt a surge of what I can only call the life force filling me from the top of my head all the way down to my toes with a remarkable vibratory power. Biologically and physically, I was utterly spent, but with a reflexive, life-giving jerk I suddenly sat bolt upright. I remained there with my eyes closed for I don't know how long — and then I began to feel a human presence off to my left, about four feet away. I opened my eyes and looked, fully expecting to see Mahalena.

It was the young girl from next door, and she was smiling. I remember she reached out and touched me on my shoulder as if to make sure I was real. I had become almost miraculously filled with new energy and life. I looked into her eyes and felt a deep yearning inside me to embrace her, embrace humanity, embrace God's creation — to finally stop judging and rejecting.

Just then a thought came blasting up from my gut, completely out of the infinite inner blue, and I heard my inner voice saying in a quiet, calm, humble tone: "God, if you'll let me live, I'll return home to my culture, and for the rest of my life just do whatever needs doing."

And, well, that's pretty much what has happened.

## FEELING CONNECTED

The Focus Phrase that most directly aims my attention at my inner spiritual center is "I feel connected with my Source." This tenth Focus Phrase is as deep as I go. Do you find that these words resonate with your past experiences of connectedness with Spirit or God (or whatever name you call God) — or is this a relatively new idea?

One of the primary universal experiences that unites all human beings deep down is a recurrent, life-changing encounter with a very real, inner spiritual presence that transcends our biologically rooted personality. Every culture has its unique name for this presence and has developed religious beliefs and priestly rituals related to this presence. But there's no doubt in my mind that the Presence itself transcends culture and is always infinitely one and the same.

One of the most radical evolutionary steps in human consciousness has been the experiential realization that there is one universal God and Creator, with whom we can commune, and from whom we can receive guidance and love, via our personal awareness. We can indeed experience oneness with the divine. The tenth Focus Phrase clearly and unequivocally declares your intent to regularly participate in this communion, to move beyond all thoughts and ideas of God and directly experience the feeling of being connected with the reality of God. "I feel connected with my Source."

Of course, when you first start working with this Focus Phrase, you may experience very little when you say these words. Fine. There's no rush, no standard to reach, no ultimate experience that these Focus Phrases will elicit each time you say them. All you do with these Focus Phrases is use them to refocus your mind in directions that have proven highly valuable.

The tenth Focus Phrase begins with the word *I* to actively involve your ego intent in the statement. The second word, *feel*, clarifies that you intend to focus on pure experience rather than an idea. The next word in the Focus Phrase clarifies what you feel: *connected*. And the final three words, *with my Source*, specify what you're focusing on. Once you've stated this lucid intent, you simply remain aware of your breathing and inner experience as you open up to see what comes to you in this eternal moment. All I can say about it is, it's always new. Go ahead and explore what happens right now as you tune in to your breathing, your whole body presence, open up to receive, and say to yourself,

*I feel connected with my Source.*

## BEYOND INNER AND OUTER

We tend to spend almost all our waking moments focused outward. Yes, we may be somewhat aware of our inner emotions and sensations here and there throughout the day. But mostly we focus our senses on what's happening around us; or we lose ourselves in memories about past sensory experiences; or we project those sensory experiences into fantasies and expectations about the future; or we lose ourselves in abstract thought about things and places and ideas primarily outside ourselves.

Meditation is about doing just the opposite, and the tenth Focus Phrase climaxes the process begun by the first. By saying, "I choose to enjoy this moment," you aim your attention inward, because enjoyment is experienced inside your body.

Breath awareness also focuses inward, on sensory events happening in your body. Likewise, when you focus on the feelings in your heart, and on your feelings toward other people and yourself, you focus inward.

When you say, "I am open to receive," you focus even deeper, on receiving intuitive and spiritual inputs. And when you say, "I feel connected with my Source," you aim your attention right at your infinite depths of being. Yes?

Well, for many years that's what I taught. But recently I've realized while meditating that, because the Source is beyond our three-dimensional material reality, we must even let go of the "inner-outer" idea when we open to connect with the Source. This ultimate Focus Phrase doesn't aim our attention at any particular place in space, so the three-dimensional concept of "inner" and "outer" models hinders the experience we want.

When you say, "I feel connected with my Source," I recommend that you stop aiming your attention entirely. Just be in the present moment, with your awareness expanded. Hold the words of the Focus Phrase in your mind and welcome whatever feeling of connection comes to you. This is the ultimate meditative and spiritual act. There is nothing deeper as far as I can see. You naturally arrive at the point where all words cease, all thoughts stop, and even the Focus Phrases fall away. Silence and peace prevail.

You've successfully led yourself to optimum consciousness for experiencing communion with your infinite, everywhere-present spiritual Source. If this is new to you, please don't become overserious; stay light with the whole idea. All you're doing is opening to feel your oneness with God. And God is simply who you already are at your infinite core, so actually you've known all along what you're going to find when you say to yourself, "I feel connected with my Source."

*Meditation is sometimes called "coming home,"*
*because you're returning your attention*
*to where you came from spiritually.*

## YOUR INNER VOICE

Early in this book, I mentioned the great value of learning to listen to your inner voice in meditation, of quieting your mind entirely and opening your heart and soul to receive inspiration and guidance from your spiritual core of being. With the ninth Focus Phrase, "I am open to receive," you arrived at the deep point in the Uplift meditation where Spirit will usually speak to you. All the previous Focus Phrases moved you toward this open, connected meditative posture, in which your ego mind is in a perfect position to listen and receive direct guidance, creativity, and inspiration from the Universal Mind. Now you've reached this point.

Many people think the purpose of meditation is simply to quiet all thoughts and remain for half an hour or longer each day in total silence. As we've seen, meditation also includes a much more active process, where the usual ego chatter is silenced so that you're able to hear, or in other ways receive, communication from your deeper self. It ultimately doesn't matter if you experience this communication as coming from God, from Spirit, from Allah, from the Tao, from the Universal Mind, from the Creator, from Jesus, or from your personal brain's integrated intuitive creative function. What's important is that, one way or another, you open up and receive.

Pretty much everyone agrees that we have an inner voice that can guide us in our lives. The trouble is that a great many people simply don't listen to that inner voice at all, because their ego voice is so constantly and loudly dominating the inner airwaves.

> *One of the primary laws of consciousness*
> *is that our inner voice cannot be heard*
> *unless and until our ego voice*
> *becomes quiet.*

Much of this book and this meditation process has been engaged in helping you quiet the constant chatter of your everyday thinking mind, so that you're in position to listen to and receive from a deeper source. The ninth Focus Phrase, as we've seen, helps you open to receive insight and inspiration, which come in various forms. The tenth Focus Phrase will sometimes take you deeper than inspiration — into a truly eternal, infinite nirvana-like state of consciousness, where your personal sense of self is temporarily entirely gone and you are entirely at one with the infinite mind of God.

When your everyday mind is quiet, and your inspirational spiritual mind is quiet as well, don't be surprised if what you experience flowing outward to you from your spiritual center has a quality entirely different from what you've experienced before. There is a radical difference between your normal thoughts, your inspired thoughts, and consciousness beyond all thoughts. Normal thoughts emerge in a linear fashion, as the ego mind works to spin concepts that describe and help manipulate reality. Inspired thoughts and creative insights flash into being in your mind instantly, as finished entities.

Direct experience of the ultimate, connected, satori state...
well, I don't want to put any words into your mind about this
experience, because it is by definition beyond words. All I can
say is, it awaits you.

## THE REAL YOU

I've already spoken about being ready to let go and willingly
give up the ego personality when death comes. This surrender
is a humble result of being openly and thankfully just another
animal on this planet — which is an honor in and of itself. To
be able to come and go — to be born, to live, and then to fade
away as new life comes: this is my experience as a mortal being.

And yet, while in deep meditation I often become aware of
another dimension of myself that is also me but not at all caught
up in the animal-ego-planetary experience. I've come to realize that, each time I move through the first ten Focus Phrases,
I'm leading myself toward the point of tuning in to this special
"spirit" dimension of consciousness, in which I will suddenly
feel one with God and eternity. My ego lets go entirely and my
personal awareness merges with a greater consciousness. I feel
at the same time here in the present moment, here before I was
born, and here after I die.

The ninth and tenth Focus Phrases will bring you to the
point where you can open and receive the flow of Spirit. They
also will bring you to the point at which you feel you're an essential, eternal, infinite part of the whole, you enter the eternal
moment and merge with the Tao.

A part of you exists beyond your conceptual ego. When
you were a two-year-old playing while no one watched, just
being yourself, and equally when you are twenty or fifty or
seventy or ninety, there is an essential, eternal you that's always

there. This is the you that opens up and receives, that feels connected.

We have the right and the freedom and the power to focus our personal attention whenever we so choose, including on the feeling of being in touch with and merging with our Source. This is our core freedom, beyond all religious law and inhibition. When we choose not to feel connected with our Source, we plunge into hell. When our ego personality starts to think it's everything there is, we become anxious and lonely. When we worship false idols and put our trust in concepts rather than spiritual truth, we become hollow and empty and descend into existential agony.

But when our ego matures and participates with our greater self, with the spiritual, eternal qualities of consciousness, then we suddenly begin to feel better, clearer, more trusting and compassionate. And when we say to ourselves each new day, or even each new hour, "I am open to receive" and "I feel connected with my Source," we live in heaven on earth. We know the truth, and the truth sets us free.

Feeling connected is what meditation is about. It's what life is about. It's what we're free to choose to feel. The first ten Focus Phrases are a solid set of mind tools that help keep you conntected with your Source.

1. I choose to enjoy this moment.
2. I feel the air flowing in and out of my nose.
3. I also feel the movements in my chest and belly as I breathe.
4. I'm aware of my whole body at once, here in this present moment.

5. I am ready to experience the feelings in my heart.
6. I let go of all my stress and worries and feel peaceful inside.
7. I accept everyone I know, just as they are.
8. I honor and love myself, just as I am.
9. I am open to receive.
10. I feel connected with my Source.

# CHAPTER ELEVEN

# CLARIFY YOUR PURPOSE

*Life is a series of natural and spontaneous changes.*
*Don't resist them — that only creates sorrow.*

*Let reality be reality*
*let things flow forward*
*in whatever way they like.*

*To the mind that is still*
*the whole universe surrenders.*

— LAO-TZU

With the eleventh Focus Phase, you begin the essential re-entry process. Perhaps you've meditated for just three minutes, or ten minutes, or half an hour, or more. At some point it's time to shift your attention outward again from deep meditation, to reemerge into your everyday world like a diver returning from the depths, bringing spiritual treasure to the surface. Your challenge is to reenter everyday life while at the same time maintaining a spiritually empowered consciousness that you can share with the world.

The eleventh Focus Phrase offers four integrated levels of decompression, each with great power to help you reengage with the world around you. In the same way that you focused your attention in order to balance and integrate the seven energy centers in your body when you began your Uplift meditation session, you will now focus your attention in order to balance and integrate the four universal foundations of human purpose.

We all have our own stated or unstated reasons for being here on earth. Except at the deepest levels of spiritual awakening, individuals without any sense of purpose tend to flounder and suffer. Everywhere, philosophers and spiritual leaders have written vast numbers of tracts on the theology and morality of purpose.

When the eleventh Focus Phrase came to me spontaneously from far beyond my philosophical mind, I was at first uncertain how to relate to the four dimensions of purpose it specifies:

I am here to serve.
    I am here to love.
        I am here to prosper.
            I am here to enjoy myself.

This list seemed at first a bit simplistic — not as deep as my philosophical notions about my underlying purpose in life. But after a few weeks of saying this Focus Phrase to myself several times each day, I began to realize the inherent psychological and spiritual wisdom of this short, succinct, and inclusive list.

My colleagues and I have enjoyed many lively discussions trying to find additional purposes to add to this list, but with no luck. Everything we thought of was adequately subsumed in the existing list. Each of the four elicitor words — *serve, love, prosper, enjoy* — evokes a powerful inclusive response, and when said one after the other they stimulate a remarkable sense of inner intent:

*I am here to serve, to love, to prosper, and to enjoy myself.*

## I AM HERE TO SERVE

I've found it interesting to notice that a great many people react negatively at first to the "here to serve" statement of purpose. In our culture, there are many negative associations with the term *to serve*. Nobody wants to be somebody's servant; this is one step away from being a slave. And to be described as servile is degrading. America is, after all, the land of the free — we are all equal, and nobody has to serve anybody else.

Yet in simple economic analysis, the opposite is true in our and all other cultures. The blunt reality is that everyone is busy serving everyone else most of the time. There is no job in which you are free from serving other people. Economics is by definition an exchange. So is any successful social or family relationship. A CEO gets up and goes to work in the morning with the specific purpose of serving the company, the shareholders, the people who will buy the company's goods, and so on. Certainly the president of the United States gets up and goes to work with the intent of being of service. The rest of us spend most of our day being of service to our employers, our families, our friends — and our deeper selves.

*The eleventh Focus Phrase*
*stimulates an integration*
*of our ego's sense of purpose*
*and our deeper spiritual purpose.*

Only with an inner sense of unified intent can we feel fulfilled in our purpose. Our ego's primary purpose is to make sure that our biological personality and organism continue to thrive as long and as enjoyably as possible. Our spiritual purpose is to bring more love, harmony, peace, and insight into the world. A successful life is one in which these two purposes are joined, which is the aim of this Focus Phrase.

It's true that the egos of many people are fear based and, as a result, greedy and selfish, and these people often try to cheat this universal give-give, win-win mutual-service equation. And many unfortunate people are getting the bum end of the deal when it comes to receiving service from others. But most of us realize, when we look at our occupations, that we earn our livings by being of service: we give, and so we receive.

At the deeper level, where being of service simply means helping others, most of us do want to help, and we do consider this a primary purpose in life. Being of service often feels so good, especially when we're serving our children in order to help them survive and grow up spiritually straight and strong.

But at the same time, most of us fight against the thought of embracing the simple phrase "I'm here to serve." As you begin to work with the eleventh Focus Phrase, all I ask is that, for the next few weeks, you regularly state this clear intent of being of service, and experience what happens inside you. Discover your buried reactions to the idea of being of service in the world. Observe them without judging yourself. The act of observing and accepting will stimulate growth in you. That's the dynamic that drives this program.

## I AM HERE TO LOVE

Most people have a fairly easy time approaching the love dimension of the eleventh Focus Phrase. It's extremely important to verbalize this intent to yourself regularly. It will directly counteract your preconditioned reactions that state the opposite — the ego is loaded with defensive, fear-based attitudes and tells you that you're a total fool to go around in love mode, trusting and being kind and compassionate to everyone you meet. The fear that blocks living in love mode comes from the worry that most people around you are probably selfish crooks who'll take advantage of you if you let your guard down even for a moment.

A contracted attitude like this might reflect past experiences, as well as the shared wisdom of your ancestors, but such an attitude doesn't relate to the true meaning of love. After all, nobody said you are here to love blindly, or that you should be loving to others but not to yourself. When you love yourself, as earlier Focus Phrases encourage you to do, you won't allow people to take advantage of you.

Love must always be balanced: it is both self-love and love for others. Jesus as psychologist stated this very clearly when he said, "Love your neighbor as you love yourself." This is a remarkable statement psychologically and spiritually, because it clarifies that first you must love yourself in order to love others. So when you say to yourself, "I'm here to love," be sure to include yourself in this mandate. That way, there will be no downside to staying in love mode all the time.

*Love* is both a cliché and a powerhouse elicitor term. When you say the word to yourself while in deep meditation, its inherent, infinite resonating power will naturally fill you.

## I AM HERE TO PROSPER

I must admit that, for quite a while, I remained mostly in denial about this particular life purpose. Except for five years or so when I was earning a regular living in San Luis Obispo, I was usually so caught up in various psychological and spiritual explorations that I never focused on career and security. Money usually flowed in as a secondary effect of what I was doing. Sometimes I had no money, and sometimes I had a lot, but prosperity wasn't a goal of mine.

Moreover, I came of age in the 1960s, during the Vietnam War, and during those early radical years I developed a strongly negative attitude toward big business and all things materialistic. At one point I even took a spiritual vow of poverty that subtly influenced my life for many years. Only during the past decade, since I started working daily with the twelve Focus Phrases, have I focused my positive intent on accumulating assets and financial security for my elder years.

Yes, my heart has opened wide to receive money. I'm not trying to sound funny here, even though those words do seem comical. After a lifetime of possessing a negative attitude toward money that did not serve me well, I realized that it had kept me from participating in certain business circles where I might otherwise have been of help. By being subtly judgmental toward people who made piles of money, many of whom were doing wonderful things with their extra funds, I had limited my expression of both love and service while also cutting myself off from the rewards of prosperity.

*We are all here on this planet to prosper,*
*and there is more than enough to go around.*

Of course it's important to regularly reconsider and redefine what we mean by *prosperity*. Science, economics, and commerce can enable us to sustain the human race on this planet beyond the subsistence level. But as a planetary society, we must learn to be ecologically responsible, and reduce and even eliminate our carbon footprints.

I recently coauthored a book called *The Conscious Capitalists* with the eminent British entrepreneur and author Jim Mellon, in which we explored how the twelve Focus Phrases can be applied to decision making in the investment and corporate leadership world. What we suggested, and what I recommend here as well, is that whenever you have a business-related decision to make, large or small, first pause and move through these twelve Focus Phrases. See what insights related to your business decision rise up from your deeper core of being. Then take action.

And each time you come to the eleventh Focus Phrase, allow your relationship with your own prosperity to evolve. Make sure, too, that you always include the other three life purposes each time you go into action to advance your prosperity. That's the key!

Prosperity entails not only financial prosperity but also a prosperous feeling about your health, your family, and your community, and about your emotional and spiritual well-being. Prosperity means that you have not only enough money and power but also enough energy, joy, playfulness, exercise, and so on — intangibles that signal genuine success in life.

## I AM HERE TO ENJOY MYSELF

As any observant therapist will tell you, and as any self-reflective priest or minister will as well, if this statement of intent is missing from a person's sense of purpose, that person will not be happy or fulfilled. In the long run, he or she will tend to dysfunction in the other three areas of life purpose.

In the old days, a great many Christians were brought up to believe they had to deny themselves pleasure in order to truly serve Christ. Protestants in particular, who subscribed to good old John Calvin's astringent teachings regarding the dangerous vice of pleasure, were seriously prejudiced against anyone caught in the sinful act of fully enjoying life. Calvin rejected all kinds of sensory pleasure, and even though the Old Testament said, "Make a joyful noise unto the Lord, all ye lands!" a great many Christians were brought up frightened to make a joyful noise. Joy itself was suspect.

Traditionally, Catholics have tended toward self-flagellation and have been keen on persecuting people who seemed to be having too much fun in life. Meditation was suspect in this regard, because most people meditate to feel better.

*I've met very few people who meditate regularly*
*who don't admit that their meditation habit reflects*
*the fact that meditation makes them feel better.*

Aside from those who fear that they're committing a sin when they feel good, everybody naturally wants to feel good. God, after all, made us that way — we're utterly fantastic pleasure-generating creatures.

We have the inherent right, according to my understanding, to seek and enjoy pleasure and happiness. If the circumstances of our employment deny us our enjoyment of the present moment as we work, it's time for a bit of revolution. If our religion uses fear-based beliefs to block our enjoyment of the present moment, I feel we have the right to challenge those beliefs. It's time for our world society to come together and establish a set of universal psychological rights that must not be violated.

We must insist that no belief system has the right to program children with fear-based beliefs that violate their ability to enjoy the present moment. The logic and justice of this is so simple and so humane — but it's been overlooked. I hope the eleventh Focus Phrase will become a mantra not only for us as individuals but for our world community as well.

In essence, why are we here on earth? It seems clear to me that we are here to serve and to love and to prosper and to enjoy ourselves. This should be a fundamental agreement we make with each other, a baseline statement of intent for the human race. If we can do so, what a wonderful world it will be!

Let's say it loud and clear:

*I am here to serve, to love, to prosper, and to enjoy myself.*

# CHAPTER TWELVE

# EMBODY COURAGE AND INTEGRITY

*Kindness in words creates confidence.*
*Kindness in thinking creates profoundness.*
*Kindness in giving creates love.*

*In dwelling, live close to the ground.*
*In thinking, keep to the simple.*
*In conflict, be fair and generous.*
*In work, do what you enjoy.*
*In governing, try not to control.*
*In family life, be completely present.*

— LAO-TZU

You have now moved through the Uplift meditative process and renewed your active participation in the world by stating your fourfold life purpose and intent: service, love, prosperity, and enjoyment of the present moment. Now it's time to go into action and bring your intent into the world.

This final step is a vital part of meditation. You've temporarily retreated to regain your senses, nurture your soul, commune with your Creator, recharge your batteries, and receive insight and guidance from your deeper self. And now once again you turn your focus outward and become an active participant in your community.

Beyond your fourfold statement of purpose, what else might you say to yourself to prepare for reentry into ordinary life? What came to me ten years ago was a Focus Phrase expressing the inner spirit of optimal engagement with the world:

*I am ready to act with courage and integrity.*

When this Focus Phrase first came to me, I wasn't sure how to relate to it. Then, through the daily and sometimes hourly act of saying this Focus Phrase to myself, I began to tap into the inherent power of these words. I encourage you to likewise be open and to explore the effect this final Focus Phrase has on your inner consciousness and your overt behavior as you open this twelfth portal step-by-step and discover the universe it awakens.

## READY FOR ACTION

The first five words, "I am ready to act," immediately shift your focus of attention from a meditative yin-passive-receptive state of consciousness to an active yang-expressive-manifesting mode of being. This is one of the primary cognitive-shifting processes of the brain.

In the Buddhist tradition (which evolved out of the more ancient Hindu tradition) there is a beautiful spiritual practice called karma yoga: the life path of spiritual action, in which you dedicate yourself to being of service to others. The word *karma* is the Sanskrit term for "to do," and *yoga* means "union with the divine." *Karma yoga* literally translates as "the path of union through action."

Karma yoga is a way of acting, thinking, and willing by which you orient yourself toward realization by letting yourself be guided by your heart, without consideration of your personal desires, likes, or dislikes. You accomplish this by acting without being attached to the fruits of your deeds. There are also a number of other traditional yoga paths that are much more inwardly focused. But balancing spiritual development with spiritual expression each and every day seems to be an ideal stance for most of us. The first ten Focus Phrases mostly aim your attention inward, as you temporarily cease all aim and turn away from the outside world to nurture your own presence. The final two Focus Phrases shift your attention to action, to karma yoga.

There will, of course, be times when you meditate and then remain in a quiet, passive, reflective mood, or perhaps go to sleep. This is perfectly fine. The twelfth Focus Phrase will prove important in motivating your readiness to act with courage and integrity, whether your next step is overt action or relaxation after the Uplift meditation.

To mention it again, the mental function that remembers to say the Focus Phrases is your ego personality, which is in charge of aiming your attention each moment. As you move through the set of Focus Phrases, you encourage the integration of your ego mind with your deeper spiritual mind, so that the voice speaking these Focus Phrases emerges from a deeper place in you. As you say the ninth and tenth Focus Phrases, this merger of your ego voice and spiritual voice reaches its maximum level, and you speak to yourself from a very deep level of consciousness. When you say, "I am ready to act," you speak from the true depths of the ancient karma yoga spirit. You are ready to act as a tuned-in, inspired spiritual being.

## COURAGE UNVEILED

The word *courage* is almost always associated with action in the face of danger. With the sixth Focus Phrase, "I let go of all my stress and worries and feel peaceful inside," you shift from fear to peace. Courage, in my understanding, is the action mode of peace.

When you choose to act with courage in the world, you're positioning yourself to participate outside the bounds of stress and anxiety. Stress and anxiety, as we've seen, tend to befuddle your mind, make you weak in the knees, decrease your compassion, and in general lessen your positive impact on the world. Choosing to act with courage does just the opposite: it empowers you to allow Spirit to act spontaneously through you, whatever you're doing.

I've recently read through medical journals to get an update on the status of psychiatric innovations for reducing anxiety and depression and, hopefully, boosting positive attributes such as courage. The news on the psychiatric front is not good. Almost a quarter of the adult population in the United States is drugged on one mood-altering chemical or another, day in and day out. But studies indicate that these drugs are only marginally effective for most people, that they induce many negative side effects, and in general reduce consciousness and separate people from their deeper spiritual presence.

Several new books, such as Gary Greenberg's *Manufacturing Depression* and Irving Kirsch's *The Emperor's New Drugs*, point out that drug companies will make over $10 billion this year selling pills that attempt to generate the same results that meditation has been proven to generate. And clinical tests simply don't verify the claims of psychiatrists and drug companies that chemical medication is the answer to emotional suffering.

There is sometimes a genetic basis for the biochemical imbalances that cause confusion, depression, and other forms of emotional suffering; but for most people, the cause of emotional suffering is not limited to malfunctioning genes. Furthermore, studies show that most people who develop what are now considered psychiatric problems recover equally well from those problems with or without drug treatment.

> *Often medication hinders natural recovery,*
> *whereas meditation can*
> *accelerate recovery.*

## LOOKING TO THE SOURCE

Anxiety, depression, weakness, and confusion seem to be running rampant these days, whereas active courage and integrity seem on the wane. Let's take a moment to look deeper into this issue, using Krishnamurti's "open inquiry" analysis: looking to see the truth and the path beyond.

Everybody's life includes a certain amount of emotional suffering. When people lose a job or spouse, or suffer some other jolt, and fall into depression, this life situation, not some mental illness or genetic defect, is usually the primary cause of their depression. And usually the natural solution to depression or anxiety (they are often inseparable) is what we've been exploring in this book. Such people need help to refocus their attention away from fearful thoughts and toward their own deeper center, so they can accept their situation, regain their inner connection with their Source, and move out into the world with renewed power, courage, and integrity.

Many professionals deny what I just said, insisting that the average person can't help himself or herself to such an extent. But this is my conclusion based on my therapist experience in encouraging the natural recovery process from depression and anxiety. Certain people in certain situations require professional help, but the majority of us do not. Most of us can release our-selves from anxiety and depression and begin acting with cour-age and integrity, with the help of two elements, 1) the passage of time, which often does heal our emotional wounds without any intervention at all; and 2) the process of learning how to con-sciously manage our own minds more positively and effectively.

With this book, and in website discussions, I hope to stim-ulate new interest in reversing the current dead-end trend of treating emotionally traumatized people as helpless victims who need medication. Let's train these people to assume full responsibility for where they focus their attention from mo-ment to moment, and enable them to shift from being victims to being victors. Because most of us periodically suffer emo-tionally as life bangs us around, this subject involves us all.

One of the most dangerous aspects of psychiatric and med-ical approaches to anxiety, depression, and so forth is that, as soon as a person starts regularly taking a mood-altering pill, that individual becomes a drugged person whose deeper spiri-tual experience has been numbed and short-circuited in the name of modern science. This form of treatment is a temporary frontal lobotomy in a pill. And in a drugged state, that person will have great difficulty recovering from the original condition and reconnecting with his or her spiritual core. Moreover, the person's ability to act with courage and integrity becomes seri-ously impaired.

We must speak out about this issue and encourage all peo-ple to courageously do something about it, both for the sake of individuals on these drugs and for the spiritual and mental in-tegrity of our culture as a whole. A culture disconnected from its spiritual source is in serious danger. Drugs cannot give us courage; courage is the choice of a clear mind. Meditation can help us attain that clear mind and heal ourselves.

Specifically, the regular use of Focus Phrases can free us so that we are able to act with clarity, compassion, courage, vision, and integrity. Doing so will enable us to maintain optimum mental health. Luckily, a growing movement throughout the world is working to bring meditation directly into the healing arena of medicine and psychiatry.

This brings us once again to the mantra that actually gets the job done: "Say it. Do it." Only by stating our intent to ourselves do we activate our clarity and power to manifest our intent. It's that simple.

## REAWAKENING INTEGRITY

The word *integrity* has several meanings in the English language. Its origins lie in ancient Latin, where the word means "whole, complete, unified." Most people now understand the word as a synonym for *honesty*, or as an assessment of a person's capacity to act within a particular code of morals or beliefs. The definition of the word *integrity* is best understood as our ability to intuitively perceive the right thing to do and then do it, even when this puts us in danger or interferes with our personal well-being or violates a cultural code of ethics.

I think of the words *courage* and *integrity* as bound together in a unit, because it takes courage to act with integrity. And in the context of the Uplift meditation process, integrity resonates with our deeper capacity to listen to our inner spiritual voice, and discover what's truly the right thing to do, and then act accordingly.

After you've moved through the first eleven Focus Phrases and tapped into some of your deeper wisdom via the meditative process, you say to yourself, "I am ready to act with courage and integrity." Then you will act powerfully, as implied by the deeper, inspired meaning of the word *integrity*.

In earlier chapters I talked considerably about the process of allowing Spirit to act through you in your daily life. Opening up to the influence of your deeper spiritual wisdom requires courage and integrity. And once you've tuned in to your deeper spiritual guidance and intuitively discovered what's right to do, the final Focus Phrase delivers the clear directive to go out and do it.

## A STEP-BY-STEP PATH

This Uplift meditation process offers a progressive daily passage through twelve portals that, each time, will lead you into new territory to discover and enjoy. During the first few weeks that you're exploring this process, you're not expected to plunge into the depths of the process. Just be sure to plunge often! As Krishnamurti so aptly put it:

*To begin to meditate*
*you must take a plunge into the water*
*not knowing how to swim.*

Raising your consciousness via your connection with your Infinite Being is an evolutionary, ever-expanding experience. As humans, we grow incrementally, step-by-step, both biologically and spiritually. Certainly we experience sudden spikes in our growth, and sometimes we have radical, instantaneous realizations. But what I offer you is an everyday, evolutionary experience in which you consciously, over and over again, focus your attention on twelve primal statements designed to evoke continuous expansion into fuller engagement with life itself.

The primary qualities that will enable you to leap forward into the newness of each moment are courage and integrity. What gives you the courage and integrity to act powerfully, both in quiet meditation and in the world, is your ongoing and expanding sense of connection with the Universal Mind. As isolated biological egos, we find it almost impossible to muster much courage or integrity. The ego tends to hide anxiety under its facade of bravado. Only by regularly immersing ourselves in Spirit can we gain the essential, deeper sense of courage and integrity.

### IN SUM

As you come to the twelfth Focus Phrase, you complete the daily or even hourly process designed to purposefully nurture your spiritual growth and positive impact on the world. You now know the full Uplift process. Be sure to take advantage of the online guided programs to help you learn the Focus Phrases by heart, and then integrate them into the various aspects of your life.

In the next chapter, I share with you four important elements related to this meditation that you can reflect on and put to use. And then it will be up to you to choose how often and how deeply you want to integrate the Uplift meditation process into your life.

Say the "courage and integrity" Focus Phrase often to yourself in the next days and weeks, either by itself or as the end of a meditation session. Experience the words' natural power to elicit a new sense of inspiration and readiness, as the integrated qualities of courage and integrity expand in you with new meaning, and offer new wisdom and empowerment:

*I am ready to act with courage and integrity.*

## THE FULL UPLIFT MEDITATION

*1. I choose to enjoy this moment.*

*2. I feel the air flowing in and out of my nose.*

*3. I also feel the movements in my chest and belly as I breathe.*

*4. I'm aware of my whole body at once, here in this present moment.*

*5. I am ready to experience the feelings in my heart.*

*6. I let go of all my stress and worries and feel peaceful inside.*

*7. I accept everyone I know, just as they are.*

*8. I honor and love myself just as I am.*

*9. I am open to receive.*

*10. I feel connected with my Source.*

*11. I am here to serve, to love, to prosper, and to enjoy myself.*

*12. I am ready to act with courage and integrity.*

(visit TappingDaily.org for daily video guidance)

# FINAL WORDS

*In yourself lies the whole world.*
*Self-knowledge has no end —*
*you don't come to an achievement*
*you don't come to a conclusion.*
*It is an endless river.*

*The intention must be to understand ourselves.*
*This is our responsibility, yours and mine.*
*When I understand myself*
*I understand you*
*and out of that understanding*
*comes love.*

— KRISHNAMURTI

As my final gesture, I return your attention to the beginning, to the air flowing in and out of your nose, and your choice to enjoy this moment. The Uplift process is best seen as an ongoing spiral that never comes to an end. Every time you return to the beginning and move through the twelve-step process, you move a step higher on the meditation spiral. You continue to gently raise your consciousness moment by moment, day by day, into the always-emerging newness that is life itself.

Traditionally, the act of repetition was often used to induce a mystical trance state. In earlier years, I greatly enjoyed chanting and ritual dancing and other repetitive spiritual processes that purposefully shifted me into a trance. But I seldom practice them anymore, because I prefer to focus my attention on the opposite of trance.

In our early research for the National Institutes of Health, we used hypnosis to induce trance states. We found that, when people are in a trance, their consciousness of and involvement with the here and now is reduced, not expanded.

*In a trance we can have remarkable experiences*
*and gain a deep sense of well-being,*
*euphoria, and transcendence of the ego.*
*But we are not quite "here" when we're in a trance.*
*I believe that raising awareness is all about*
*being more distinctly here,*
*not less distinctly here.*

When I suggest that you return to the beginning of the Uplift meditation process and repeat the twelve Focus Phrases over and over to yourself during the next weeks, months, and years, and very possibly throughout your entire life, I don't mean you should do this to induce a trance state. In the opposite direction, the design of the Uplift procedure allows you ample time, right after you say a phrase, to enter into a unique, emerging experience. Even if you say a new Focus Phrase with every new exhalation, each time you then inhale, the words of the Focus Phrase will positively affect your consciousness, awakening and expanding your awareness.

I've written this book so that you can return to parts of it over and over as you get more involved in each dimension of the meditation process. Every time you reread a chapter, especially if you're aware of your breathing as you read (are you now?), new insights will emerge to inspire and guide you through the Uplift process.

Following this final chapter, you'll find a section that introduces you to an assortment of online audio and video presentations with meditation guidance that will also prove especially helpful as you learn this process by heart. My hope is that, even twenty or thirty years from now, we'll still have a lively, ongoing online community and ever-expanding support system at www.johnselby.com. We shall see!

## EVERY MOMENT IS MEDITATION

As you begin integrating these Focus Phrases into your life, you can insert the Uplift meditation into your routine in three main ways.

First, see if you can discipline yourself to pause once or twice a day, and take five minutes to half an hour off from your usual busy life to use the twelve Focus Phrases to move yourself into a deep consciousness. During this time, the natural spiritual balancing process will recharge your energy centers, healing your body and emotions wherever necessary and allowing your inner voice to bring you new insight and guidance.

Second, pause often for shorter Uplifts of just two to three minutes. During these moments you can move quickly through four or more of the Focus Phrases, taking just one to two breaths for each. This is an optimum approach when you're busy at work, commuting, or otherwise out in the world doing your thing. It's amazing what can happen in two to three minutes, once you become adept at the process.

Third, each day choose one of the twelve Focus Phrases to be your constant companion that day. When you pause and reflect on the Focus Phrase list, you'll intuitively notice that one of the phrases seems especially important and lingers in your mind. Allow this one to remain present in your awareness throughout the day, like a song that sticks in your head for hours. The impact on your life can be dramatic. At my website you'll find games to help you randomly choose your Focus Phrase for the day.

Remember that meditation isn't something to do now and then during the day. Meditation means being as aware as possible, as often as possible, and it is something to do every moment.

*Starting right now, there is nothing keeping you*
*from being in a meditative state*
*every moment of every day.*
*Just choose to consciously*
*enjoy each new moment*
*as you stay aware of the air*
*flowing in and out of your nose.*
*Here you are!*

Of course, the ideal of constantly being in that expanded state of mind is compromised by the natural tendency of our ego minds to enter everyday "head-trip" thinking mode and, in so doing, let go of breath awareness. I still lose awareness of my breathing many times each day, but because I honor and love myself just as I am, this doesn't really bother me. I actually enjoy all aspects of my mortal experience, including the ones that tend to pull me away from my conscious breathing now and then.

Deep down, though, I hunger to be highly aware in the here and now, because this is where I feel most alive and creative and loving. And this hunger for maintaining a spiritual sense of connectedness with the divine motivates me to stay aware of my breathing as much as I can each day.

I look forward to hearing online about your own experiences in this regard. I'll do my best to keep a chat forum or Facebook type of communication going, where we can share our ideas, questions, insights, and experiences.

## BEYOND SEEKING: FINDING

With so many new, exciting things in the meditation world to choose from, many people these days find themselves caught chronically searching for that one special belief, meditation, teacher, or self-help book that will finally be perfect for them. There's always been a universal tendency to get lost in the hunt — and many people are actually afraid of finding what they're looking for. Instead, they dabble a bit in a particular tradition, meditative process, or self-help procedure, take a quick taste, and then, for one reason or another, abandon that particular method or book or teacher and go off looking for another external stimulus. This may be a low-risk approach to spiritual growth, but unfortunately it's also a low-yield approach.

*If you're ready to stop looking
and finally find what you yearn for,
perhaps your seeking days are over.*

This Uplift meditation process is not actually designed for seekers. It's designed for people who want to find what they're looking for and settle into the next vital phase of their spiritual evolution. Krishnamurti said:

*The moment you follow someone*
*you cease to follow truth.*
*In yourself lies the whole world —*
*and if you are willing to look within*
*and discover your own truth*
*the door is always ready before you*
*and the key in your hand.*

In all humbleness and to the best of my knowledge, no other techniques or forms of guidance aside from these twelve Focus Phrases are necessary in order to find and nurture your own spiritual center and your ever-evolving sense of intimate contact with the divine. I've now offered practical guidance on how to look and learn. The rest is in your hands. As one Zen aphorism says, there's nowhere to go, nothing to do. Whatever this is, this is it. Just stay aware!

## MANIFEST YOUR INNER DESIRE

Many times every day, each of us employs our power of intent to manifest what we desire or need in life. I've written extensively about this in *Tapping the Source*. Let me offer a few insights into how the Uplift process you're learning here will also help you in everyday material and spiritual manifestation.

As the Uplift meditation process quiets your mind and you enter into a "being" state of consciousness, very often you'll naturally tap into deep desires and yearnings, which will in turn lead, step-by-step, to ideas, visions, actions, and manifestations in your life. In fact one of the great values of temporarily quieting the mind and putting aside your habitual routine is that you shift into position to connect with your spiritual needs and desires.

*In meditation,*
*once you connect with*
*and honor an unfulfilled passion,*
*you'll be able to tap*
*remarkable manifestation powers*
*to fulfill that passion.*

One of America's great early spiritual teachers, whom I talk about at length in *Tapping the Source*, was a fellow from the Midwest called Charles Haanel. A hundred years ago, he explained clearly that, if you learn to enter into silence, you can tap directly into the Universal Mind, discover your true yearnings, and receive creative guidance, insight, and empowerment that inspire you to manifest your dreams.

When you fully quiet your mind in the Uplift meditation, and listen to your deeper, inner voice, you will, I assure you, begin to discover what you really yearn for in order to feel fulfilled. When you say to yourself, "I am open to receive," and then connect with the divine wisdom of the universe by saying, "I feel connected with my Source," don't be surprised if you encounter strong passions and new ideas. These in turn will bring you creative visions that lead you to manifest something unique and valuable.

What really happens in the Uplift meditation process is that you open up to allow Spirit to help you manifest your deeper presence and purpose on this planet. Each time you move through the Uplift process, or any other meditation technique that quiets the mind and opens you up to spiritual guidance, you connect with what you yearn for at your core, which then stimulates the evolution of your spiritual consciousness. If that isn't the heart of manifestation, I don't know what is.

## SHARING YOUR MOMENT

My wife, Birgitta, and I have been exploring these twelve Focus Phrases together ever since they appeared in our lives a decade ago. For fifteen years before that, since we first came together, we'd been exploring similar "intent statements" that influenced not only our inner personal experience but also our shared experience of each other. I'd like to end this book by talking about the power of the Uplift meditation to influence your relationships.

What actually happens when people begin exploring these Focus Phrases together? When two or more people choose to focus on the same thing at the same time — whether they are a couple in an intimate relationship, a family, a church group, a school, a business organization, or people engaged in some other social situation — a unique power is unleashed.

In the PEAR research I mentioned earlier, we saw how one person focusing his or her intent on a random-number generator elicited positive results demonstrating the physical power of focused intent. The PEAR researchers then asked two people who didn't know each other to focus their power of intent on the same machine at the same time — and this doubled the effect.

Then the researchers got really daring and used couples who were in love — and instead of the expected doubling of effect, it was between five and six times greater. These results thrilled me no end because I've always felt that some special power emanates from two people who are in love when they together focus their attention to accomplish something.

Certainly the sexual act of creating a new being generates a remarkable creative charge. And in the creation of the family home, likewise, the power of intent of a loving couple generates a unique, life-sustaining atmosphere. With or without the sexual dimension, when you bring something like the Uplift meditation process into a relationship where two or more people choose to focus their power of intent on a common cause, the results will predictably have great value.

In daily life I often gaze at Birgitta while also aware of my breathing and physical presence, and she looks back at me with that particular brightness in her eyes that lets me know she's also in tune with her breathing and whole-body presence. At a primal level of awareness, we're in the same place. The fact that we regularly share this particular spiritual state of consciousness is the foundation of our relationship.

In this same spirit, if you have a sexual partner, you'll find (as I point out in *Let Love Find You*) that during a sexual interlude you can dramatically deepen your intimate relationship by doing nothing at all besides lying quietly side by side as you both move through the first few Focus Phrases. When you pause like this to quiet your minds, let your bodies and emotions come fully into the present moment, and then expand your awareness naturally to include the other person, you don't have to "do" anything at all. Spirit will begin to move you together, heart to heart, body to body, soul to soul.

In a different context, groups without any sexual overtones can begin a gathering by having everyone move through the Focus Phrases together. This will beautifully and powerfully heighten the ensuing group experience. Creative ideas will flash at deeper levels, and cooperative relating will increase, as the group receives a special high-order impetus to manifest its intent in the world.

*Whenever we quiet our minds together*
*and open up to receive guidance*

*and insight in our lives from a higher source,*
*we do come together in greater consciousness*
*of what we're all sharing, right here, right now.*
*My great hope for the future*
*is that we will more and more learn to tap into*
*our shared spiritual experience.*

Meanwhile, you now have all the consciousness tools you need in order to regularly pause and uplift your spirit and further wake up your higher presence. It's time for me to stop talking, and allow you to take full responsibility for applying these twelve Focus Phrases daily or even hourly in your life, as you feel guided by Spirit.

As a final suggestion, I do encourage you to reread each chapter at least once during the next weeks, as you move deeper into the power and pleasure of each Focus Phrase. And I look forward to continuing our relationship online at www. johnselby.com, which is also linked to www.TappingDaily.org, where I will regularly be posting new teaching videos and written insights into this Uplift process.

A poem from my formative years just popped into mind, and I think it's a most fitting thought to end this book with — the famous lines from T. S. Eliot that still ring so true:

*We shall not cease from exploration*
*And the end of all our exploring*
*Will be to arrive where we started*
*And know the place for the first time.*

*Life should be lived naturally*
*according to the laws of nature.*
*Cooking or washing your clothes,*
*going to work or making love —*
*any activity can become meditation.*

*When meditation spreads over all your life*
*it becomes just part of you,*
*like breathing,*
*like your heartbeat.*
*This is the essential practice of meditation.*

—— OSHO

# FOR FURTHER EXPLORATION

## ONLINE TRAINING AND DVD PROGRAMS

For the past five years, my partner, Birgitta, and I have worked steadily to produce online and multimedia training programs that are either free or inexpensive, easy to access, and consistently effective in helping you master and continue with the Uplift meditation process. These programs are continually evolving and expanding, and as long as the electricity flows and the Internet glows, we intend to continue developing the very best tools, because there are times when a guiding voice can be very helpful as you learn to go deeper into meditation and spiritual awakening.

We intend to maintain the following Web addresses as our long-term training and contact links. We'll need to offset our expenses by charging a bit for some of the programs, but we'll also keep many of them up and running for free. See you there!

www.johnselby.com
www.youtube.com/selby2424
www.tappingdaily.org

## ONLINE PERSONAL COACHING AND LIVE SEMINARS

If you would like some personal online coaching, or perhaps an online meditation training seminar, please go to one of my websites mentioned above and find a program that suits your needs. As time permits, Birgitta and I will continue to do our best to also get out and lead live meditation-training seminars in Hawaii, on the mainland, and in Europe. Please email us at one of our websites if you would like to host a live seminar in your region, or if you want information on when and where you can attend one of our meditation workshops.

## FURTHER READING AND RESOURCES

The websites posted above will also guide you to other books on meditation that you might find useful. We will regularly update the websites to let you know about new media resources that are being developed that you might find helpful.

# ABOUT THE AUTHOR

John Selby is an author, executive counselor, videographer, researcher, marketing consultant, and awareness-management pioneer. He is the author of over two dozen self-help, spiritual-growth, business-success, and psychology books, published in fourteen languages with over half a million books in print.

Early in his career he conducted mind-management research for NIH and the New Jersey Neuro-Psychiatric Institute and explored innovative approaches to stress relief, insomnia treatment, cognitive shifting, and short-form meditation. Educated at Princeton University, UC Berkeley, the Graduate Theological Union, and the Radix Institute, John spent two decades working as a therapist and mindfulness coach while continuing with research into more effective cognitive methods for quieting the mind and maintaining a more alert, relaxed, enjoyable present-moment focus.

www.johnselby.com

## YOUR DAILY UPLIFT MEDITATION

1. *I choose to enjoy this moment.*

2. *I feel the air flowing in and out of my nose.*

3. *I also feel the movements in my chest and belly as I breathe.*

4. *I'm aware of my whole body at once, here in this present moment.*

5. *I am ready to experience the feelings in my heart.*

6. *I let go of all my stress and worries and feel peaceful inside.*

7. *I accept everyone I know, just as they are.*

8. *I honor and love myself just as I am.*

9. *I am open to receive.*

10. *I feel connected with my Source.*

11. *I am here to serve, to love, to prosper, and to enjoy myself.*

12. *I am ready to act with courage and integrity.*

(visit TappingDaily.org for daily video guidance)

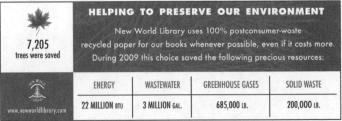

**HELPING TO PRESERVE OUR ENVIRONMENT**

7,205 trees were saved

New World Library uses 100% postconsumer-waste recycled paper for our books whenever possible, even if it costs more. During 2009 this choice saved the following precious resources:

www.newworldlibrary.com

| ENERGY | WASTEWATER | GREENHOUSE GASES | SOLID WASTE |
| --- | --- | --- | --- |
| 22 MILLION BTU | 3 MILLION GAL. | 685,000 LB. | 200,000 LB. |

Environmental impact estimates were made using the Environmental Defense Fund Paper Calculator @ www.papercalculator.org.